Advancing the Development of Urban School Superintendents Through Adaptive Leadership

Based on a case study of urban school superintendents in a leadership development program, this book offers a concrete demonstration of how adaptive leadership is applied and learned. Blending the theory of adaptive leadership with the practice of urban school superintendents, this book also utilizes the analytic lens of transformative learning as developed by Jack Mezirow.

Sarah Chace is assistant professor of Leadership Studies at Christopher Newport University, USA.

Routledge Research in Educational Leadership series

Books in This Series

Political Philosophy, Educational Administration and Educative Leadership
Reynold Macpherson

Educational Administration and Leadership
Theoretical Foundations
Edited by David Burgess and Paul Newton

Indigenous Leadership in Higher Education
Edited by Robin Starr Minthorn and Alicia Fedelina Chávez

Student Voice and School Governance
Distributing Leadership to Youth and Adults
Mark Brasof

Leading for Change
Race, Intimacy and Leadership on Divided University Campuses
Jonathan Jansen

Restoring Justice in Urban Schools
Disrupting the School-to-Prison Pipeline
Anita Wadhwa

Generational Identity, Educational Change, and School Leadership
Corrie Stone-Johnson

Educational Leadership in Becoming
Nuraan Davids and Yusef Waghid

Educational Leadership for Transformation and Social Justice
Narratives of Change in South Africa
John Ambrosio

The Hermeneutics of Jesuit Leadership
The Meaning and Culture of Catholic-Jesuit Presidents
Maduabuchi Leo Muoneme

Advancing the Development of Urban School Superintendents Through Adaptive Leadership
Sarah Chace

Advancing the Development of Urban School Superintendents Through Adaptive Leadership

Sarah Chace

LONDON AND NEW YORK

First published 2019
by Routledge

2 Park Square, Milton Park, Abingdon, Oxfordshire OX14 4RN
52 Vanderbilt Avenue, New York, NY 10017

Routledge is an imprint of the Taylor & Francis Group, an informa business

First issued in paperback 2020

Copyright © 2019 Taylor & Francis

The right of Sarah Chace to be identified as author of this work has been asserted by her in accordance with sections 77 and 78 of the Copyright, Designs and Patents Act 1988.

All rights reserved. No part of this book may be reprinted or reproduced or utilised in any form or by any electronic, mechanical, or other means, now known or hereafter invented, including photocopying and recording, or in any information storage or retrieval system, without permission in writing from the publishers.

Notice:
Product or corporate names may be trademarks or registered trademarks, and are used only for identification and explanation without intent to infringe.

Library of Congress Cataloguing-in-Publication Data
Names: Chace, Sarah, author.
Title: Advancing the development of urban school
  superintendents through adaptive leadership / By Sarah Chace.
Description: First edition. | New York : Routledge, [2019] |
  Series: Routledge research in educational leadership |
  Includes bibliographical references.
Identifiers: LCCN 2018056763 | ISBN 9781138672352 (hardback) |
  ISBN 9781315562568 (ebk)
Subjects: LCSH: School superintendents—United States. |
  Educational leadership—United States. | Urban schools—United
  States—Administration. | Education, Urban—United States. |
  School management and organization—United States.
Classification: LCC LB2831.72 .C47 2019 | DDC 371.2/011—dc23
LC record available at https://lccn.loc.gov/2018056763

ISBN: 978-1-138-67235-2 (hbk)
ISBN: 978-0-367-66136-6 (pbk)

Typeset in Sabon
by Apex CoVantage, LLC

This book is dedicated to all those who created, offered, and defined a holding environment for its writing. In particular, to R.E.F.—who knows what a holding environment is and must be.

And to the memory of Sue Williamson, 1946–2006.

Contents

List of Figure and Tables viii
Foreword ix
Preface xi
Acknowledgments xiv

1 Introduction 1
2 Participating Superintendents: Profiles in Leadership—and Survival 11
3 Description of the Program for Leading Superintendents (PLS) 29
4 How Participants Remembered PLS 47
5 Sifting Through the Narrative 90
6 Conclusions and Recommendations for Future Research 114

Index 128

Figure and Tables

Figure

3.1	PLS Sample Schedule	41

Tables

2.1	Demographic Distribution of Sample	13
2.2	Student Demographic Information for Superintendents' Districts	13
2.3	Findings for Superintendents' Contexts	25
4.1	Participant Responses: How Adaptive Leadership Concepts Affected Aspects of Superintendent Context	51
4.2	Participant Responses: Findings on Shifts in Perspective	73
4.3	Transformative Learning: Steps Taken	78
4.4	Superintendents' Perspectives on PLS as Professional Development	82
4.5	PLS as Professional Development	83
5.1	Summary of Changes Reported by Superintendents as a Result of Learning	92
5.2	Analysis of Superintendents' Departures From Districts	95
5.3	Reported Changes: Near and Far Transfer of Learning	109

Foreword

A really tough job. That's the only fair way to describe being an urban school superintendent today. Fierce community politics. Combative boards of education. Deep-seated racial conflict. Multiple constituencies with competing and unrealistic demands. It's little wonder that the job turnover for urban superintendents is so high.

In this environment, it's worth asking what universities can do to maximize the chances that good people are able to survive—even thrive—in these near-impossible positions. What we do know is that there is no "one best way" to prepare people for these positions. What we also know is that there is a dearth of information about innovative programs designed to meet the special needs of the urban superintendent.

Enter Sarah Chace's informative new book, which helps fill that gap. While much has been written about both school superintendents and leadership, thus far there has not been a detailed empirical study of an especially promising program designed for urban school superintendents—namely, a program based upon the theory and pedagogical methods of adaptive leadership.

Indeed, this book provides a unique portrait of a leadership program for a group of high-profile urban superintendents, coming into the program during the advent of No Child Left Behind. The book offers a cogent analysis of a program that has never (to my knowledge) been replicated. Writing as a participant-observer in the program, and the lead administrator, Sarah Chace captures the reflections of a handful of educators on their experience of a radical new approach to leadership—one that is highly experiential, provocative, and personal.

The book is aimed at practitioners interested in adaptive leadership principles applied in real time, at educators dealing with complex urban systems, and at anyone who has an interest in the politics of race, class, and public education. It is also aimed at scholars of leadership who are seeking empirical studies of a relatively recent formulation of the concept "leadership."

The book is important and worth reading for these reasons: first, it offers genuine empirical research on a highly theoretical leadership approach; second, it is readable and accessible while possessing scholarly gravitas; and, finally, it offers grant-making philanthropies an example of a highly successful, risk-taking leadership program.

Jerome T. Murphy
Harold Howe II Professor of Education Emeritus
Dean Emeritus, Harvard Graduate School of Education

Preface

In a way, the arc of the Program for Leading Superintendents' (PLS) existence, which is the subject of this book, mirrored the trajectory of my own professional life. Ten years prior to its launch, I had entered my own teaching career in K–12 education, beginning with a stint teaching at a New York City private school similar to the one I attended decades before and ending with my tenure as a founding teacher at one of the first charter schools to be established in Massachusetts. My love of education runs deep. To this day, tears come to my eyes when I so much as read a newsletter from my alma mater. Yet I have been keenly aware of the privilege I embody, having attended private schools for all but four short months of my formative years of schooling.

Those months remain in memory as a fog of time when I was virtually uneducated in a moldering public school in Cambridge. (My younger sister, then in the second grade, was one of two children in her class who could read.) As it happened, circumstances allowed us to return to New York and back into the fold of our former all-girls private school, where the classes were small, the teachers committed and amply supported, and the population less troubled—at least, when it came to socioeconomics. Perhaps those early impressions of the educational disparities in our society are what ignited in me an enduring passion for education—good education—as a human right and not a rare privilege.

Initially, I had thought that the movement for independent public schools (charter schools) might serve as a solution for the gap between those with means and those who were continuously underserved in our society. By the time I left my teaching job in Massachusetts, however, my eyes were opened to the political challenges surrounding such an intervention. This recognition—that the larger structure surrounding education (indeed, any enterprise) beginning with its leadership will make or break an institution—was critical to my entry into the world of leadership studies in 2001. It was through this somewhat disillusioned departure from K–12 at the turn of the century that I found myself, one year later, embarked upon the ambitious adventure of changing outcomes in education by working to influence the leadership practices at the top of the authority pyramid—with superintendents. For such was PLS's goal.

This book represents an extraordinary moment in the history of education in the US. Following a decade of standards-based reform, and on the cusp of the now infamous No Child Left Behind (NCLB) Act (passed into law during the first months of the George W. Bush Administration), a visionary philanthropic foundation agreed to fund a somewhat radical approach to leadership for a group of a dozen carefully chosen superintendents. Between them, these 12 individuals represented some of the most complex urban districts in the US, with geographical representation spanning the country. As a pilot program linked to a larger funding initiative, this foundation could afford to underwrite a leadership training program of remarkable breadth and scope. As someone with familiarity with the current issues of K–12 education who had become an avid student of adaptive leadership, I was brought in to consult to as well as manage this program for its duration. To my knowledge, little has been done in the way of leadership training programs for educational leaders that has had as much potential to shift systemic values as has PLS.

This leadership training program not only reflected aspects of my own life, it also reflected in microcosm the competing interests and complexities of the very system it sought to improve. For in its execution PLS's noble aims were curtailed by the substance of the system into which it attempted to intervene. However powerful the foundation and the program were, the systems in which it took place and attempted to change proved to be stronger.

For not only did PLS reflect the system in which it intervened in K–12, but the undertaking of the program also reflected the micro-politics of the institution in which it was housed. From the moment the program began, competing interests of researchers and practitioners brought to a stalemate a number of efforts at formal research on this program. (To my knowledge, the dissertation upon which this book is based contains the most robust form of research that has occurred since its inception and termination.) Competing interests at the underwriting foundation ended up compromising the original vision that sparked the program. And, in many cases, as these pages will reveal, the participating superintendents were powerless in the face of the larger systemic forces in which they immediately operated.

And yet, as Martin Luther King, Jr., once famously proclaimed, "the arc of history is long." Echoing MLK, Senator Robert Kennedy offered the vision of a "ripple of hope . . . which can sweep down the mightiest walls of oppression and resistance." While both of these iconic American figures addressed the civil rights struggles of the last century—rights that are, it must be said, still unattained by all—I use their words to illustrate what is perhaps a subtler means of oppression: the oppression of a system that will not and does not change. I am speaking here not of particular public education policy (though that needs fixing); rather, I am articulating the fundamental need for a shift in our society, where the job of teacher is seen as an esteemed profession, not as a second-class career—as it is in so many quarters.

I will close with a small anecdote to support my point. One afternoon many years ago I was sitting on the back porch of a friend of mine, sharing the news of my decision to attend a graduate school program at a prestigious university. This person had largely known me as a struggling teacher within the fraught atmosphere of the charter school. "Wow," she said, "Now you're doing something serious." How I wish she had meant the opposite: that a departure from a prestigious institution to serve as a teacher might be seen as the more serious course of action. When that day comes, the time of teacher as leader and leader as teacher will have truly arrived.

Acknowledgments

While the writing of this book has felt, at times, acutely solitary, there are many people who deserve my thanks and acknowledgment for being a part of the process, at whatever distance. One of the first people I should mention is Bobbi D'Alessandro, who encouraged me long ago to undertake a study of this unique group of urban school superintendents. Her interest sustained me more than she may know. My initial dissertation advisor (later committee member), Victoria Marsick, was similarly influential as she offered me her own deeply creative ideas on Billy Joel and Twyla Tharp as a way of helping me to see how a book could emerge from the study I undertook at Teachers College. My editors at Routledge—Matthew Friberg and, in the early stages of my proposal, Christina Chronister—have offered me unwavering support, and I am thankful for the seriousness and appreciation they have shown for this work.

Friends—all friends—and family who took a genuine interest in this enterprise deserve recognition. In particular, I wish to mention Natalie Dykstra, who along with being my champion has also been my mentor. Shepley Metcalf has supported me in ways that go beyond the reach of so generously offering me a space in which to "read, write, think" in Cambridge. In doing so, she has given me access to environments in which this work has been allowed to thrive. Megan Tschannen-Moran has been wonderfully helpful as well, and I am grateful for her friendship. Kathy Walker has been unflagging in her enthusiasm for this project. Last, but certainly not least, my cousin Victoria Cobb has on two occasions offered me her home in upstate New York at critical junctures, where I could be on retreat from my usual surroundings. I am also grateful to her husband, Emrys Westacott, who offered critical advice at the advent of this undertaking. The home of the Cobb-Westacotts has served as a salutary holding environment for me; for two summers the proximity to Alfred University was a gift, and through it I met Leah Houk. Leah became a delightful friend as well as editorial assistant par excellence for me. Thank you, Leah, for all you have done. I truly could not have done this without you.

In Cambridge, I am grateful to the Harvard Libraries, which continue to offer their scholarly alums generous support that has made all the difference. In Boston and away from it, Brita Heimarck has been an insightful partner in scholarship.

Finally, I wish to acknowledge that some parts of this book appeared, often in a different form, as parts of my dissertation, "Learning Leadership: A Case Study on Influences of a Leadership Training Program on the Practices of One Group of Urban School Superintendents." Any errors that appear in this work are entirely my own.

SVC, 13 July 2018, Cambridge, Massachusetts

1 Introduction

Sometimes characterized as "deer in the headlights," freshly minted urban school superintendents often experience disorientation as they adjust to the transition from the role of instructional manager to that of adept politician. The traditional journey from expert teacher to school principal to district superintendent does not necessarily prepare education professionals for contending with the politics of the current educational climate of high-stakes testing, budget cuts, and violence in schools. The environment in which an urban school superintendent finds herself is often confusing to the point of paralysis.

In addition to navigating an increasingly complex and diverse educational landscape, school superintendents have had to contend with a widely perceived diminishment of trust in the authority of many traditional institutions, including authorities in schools. As Megan Tschannen-Moran writes,

> We live in an era in which all of our social institutions and their leaders have come under unprecedented scrutiny. As a result, trust has become increasingly difficult for leaders to earn and maintain in our complex and rapidly changing world. This trend away from trust poses a special challenge for school leaders because trust is so vital for schools in fulfilling their fundamental mission of teaching students to be engaged and productive citizens.
>
> (Tschannen-Moran, 2014, p. x)

One way that trust in school authority figures can be repaired is through the careful training of those authority figures in proven leadership techniques. In the early 2000s, a philanthropic foundation made the decision to invest in the leadership education of a select group of urban school superintendents with a radical, experiential approach based on Heifetz's model of adaptive leadership (Guilleux, 2011; Heifetz, 1994; Heifetz, Grashow, & Linsky, 2009; Heifetz & Laurie, 1997; Heifetz & Linsky, 2002, 2004; O'Brien, 2016; Parks, 2005). The story of these superintendents' learning journeys is the story that forms the narrative arc of this book.

Each of the eight program participants who participated in the study—three women and five men—traveled a distinct path to the superintendency. (Due to restrictions on the study of human subjects, five of the eight will be discussed here.) At the time of their participation in the leadership training program, they ranged from freshly minted to veteran superintendents—all of whom were in charge of troubled urban districts.

These superintendents had disparate challenges with which to contend, yet the national political context in which they operated was a common one. At the advent of their leadership training program, the second Bush administration's signature education law, NCLB had just been passed by Congress with robust bipartisan support. The new legislation focused on standardized testing and other quantifiable measures of improved student achievement (Lemann, 2001). While the legislation was met with cautious optimism by some, anecdotal evidence suggests that the implementation was harrowing for schools across the nation, and perhaps especially so for urban districts.

At the time of the first convening of the leadership training program, less than a year had passed since 9/11, and the US economy had recently suffered a downturn. New York City was on the cusp of a massive restructuring effort in its department of education under the aegis of former Microsoft litigator Joel Klein and a newly elected mayor, billionaire businessman and philanthropist Michael Bloomberg. Atlanta was under the stewardship of Beverly Hall, who would later be indicted on racketeering charges for a massive cheating scandal that occurred midway through her tenure. It was in the shadow of this sweeping new educational legislation, economic uncertainty, and international political instability that the Program for Leading Superintendents emerged.

PLS evolved into a two-year executive program with methods based largely on a graduate course for aspiring leaders, initially pioneered by Harvard Kennedy School's Dr. Ronald Heifetz. The program included experiential learning and case presentations, and the training centered around the tenets of adaptive leadership and transformative learning. As the administrative manager of PLS, I developed relationships with each of the participating superintendents, and my doctoral dissertation research, on which this book is based, consisted of interviews with 8 of the 12 participants.

This study culled the learning outcomes for the PLS participants that took place both during and after the program. In particular, I examined the application of the main concepts of adaptive leadership to real-world problems that the superintendents encountered for the duration of the two-year PLS program (May 2002–May 2004), and in the six or seven years that had elapsed since the program's termination. (My interviews took place in the fall of 2010 and the spring and summer of 2011.)

I analyzed the interview material through the lens of transformative learning (Mezirow et al., 2000) and the perspectives of the theory of transfer of training (cf. Holton & Baldwin, 2003), as well as that of linguistic theory. The purpose of the study was to add to the knowledge base of adaptive leadership, about which little is empirically known,[1] and to contribute to the field of adult learning.

The driving question of this study had to do with whether and how the superintendents implemented the concepts taught during the PLS program. Some of the superintendents' learning journeys clearly showcased the adaptive leadership concepts, while others did so less obviously—and some not at all. All of the superintendents, however, appeared to have used at least one of the numerous concepts taught in the program in their professional work, and some used the concepts in their personal lives as well.

Organization of the Book

This book is organized into six chapters, each of which builds upon the last. The reader will find that I have inserted myself into the narrative in ways that depart from some traditional scholarly works; I have done so because this book is in part a recollection of my own experience, and because I believe my own perspective enriches the content.

Chapter 1: Introduction

Here I describe how PLS came into being, including the evolution of adaptive leadership as an increasingly popular area of study within the sub-discipline of leadership studies. I discuss the broader context of the program, including the political landscape of school reform in the early 21st century. Finally, I offer key definitions for the tenets of adaptive leadership.

Chapter 2: Participating Superintendents: Profiles in Leadership—and Survival

Chapter 2 describes the experiences of each of the participating superintendents. Professional biographies of the women and men (identifying details disguised) highlight their own views of their development as leaders and in particular their narratives of themselves as leaders during and following their participation in PLS.

Chapter 3: Description of the Program for Leading Superintendents (PLS)

This chapter offers an in-depth description of how the program unfolded, including how the teaching sessions were run and how the superintendents were affected by the program.

Chapter 4: How Participants Remembered PLS

This chapter weaves together the superintendents' recollections of the program from the interviews I conducted over the course of a year. The voices of each of the superintendents add texture to the narrative and ground my research in their lived experience.

Chapter 5: Sifting Through the Narrative

This chapter views the data gleaned from superintendents' recollection of PLS through the conceptual lenses of adaptive leadership and transformative learning, as well as linguistic theory.

Chapter 6: Conclusions and Recommendations for Future Research

In this chapter, I draw some conclusions about the data and discuss clusters of themes centering around topics such as race, gender, and years of experience. I propose that future research be undertaken using theories of "transfer of training" (Holton & Baldwin, 2003) as well as creating new strands of research via cross-pollination of existing theory.

Defining Adaptive Leadership

"Of all the hazy and confounding areas in social psychology," wrote Warren Bennis in 1959, "leadership theory undoubtedly contends for top nomination" (p. 260). Thirty years later, Joseph Rost made the same complaint, devoting half of his own seminal writing on leadership in *Leadership for the Twenty-First Century* (1991/1993) to the argument as to why scholars of management and leadership had eschewed the task of defining the term "leadership."

One of the critical contributions Heifetz made with his introduction of the adaptive leadership model in the 1980s was that of creating a series of definitions and distinctions in terms. Most importantly, perhaps, he articulated a clear line between the notions of authority and leadership.

In this theory, leadership is defined as an action rather than as a static position. An individual's sense of when and how to exercise leadership is connected with their sense of a group's readiness for intervention. The notion of "intervention" (Heifetz, 1994; Heifetz & Linsky, 2002; Williams, 2005) is rooted in the theory of group dynamics (Bion, 1961; Smith & Berg, 1987). The purpose of leadership is to intervene in a group dynamic in order to move it toward progress.

Any group engaged in the process of shifting values, beliefs, and assumptions will, in the course of that struggle, be likely to divide into factions embodying disparate values. The more firmly these values are held, the stiffer the resistance to change. Such resistance causes fragmentation instead of the flexibility of adaptation. Fragmentation often occurs when there is a perception of a zero-sum game—a perception under which most factions operate. The values of some members of a community may shift and others may not, depending on the losses they perceive to be occurring in their group (Smith & Berg, 1987).

Examples of adaptive leadership cluster around social justice movements such as the civil rights movement in the US, as well as healthcare scenarios, and certain political leadership (Heifetz, 1994). These examples offer illustrations of groups that engage in what Heifetz calls the "adaptive challenge," which is located in the gap between a group's aspirations and its lived realities. Thus, the adaptive challenge that emerged for the Catholic Church at the turn of the 21st century resided in the enormous gap between its aspiration to treat children and young people with devotion and respect, and the lived reality for many of the sex-abuse scandal perpetrated on them by the authority figures of priests.

A partial list of additional definitions and distinctions in adaptive leadership terminology follows. These terms formed the nine conceptual pillars of PLS. The definitions are based on those provided by Heifetz (1994), Heifetz and Linsky (2002), and Heifetz and Sinder (1991a; 1991b). The terms are listed in the order of frequency with which the superintendents in PLS discussed them during their interviews.

1. *Diagnosing Stakeholder Values.* This concept has to do with the theory that individuals and groups cluster around values, notions of what represents their highest worth to them. For example, the all-male tradition of a "finals club" at a prestigious university might represent the value of a centuries-old tradition and belongingness to a certain sector of society. Heifetz has often said that adversaries are "ninety percent representing their factions and ten percent jerks" (Heifetz, personal communication, May 2001). In numerous classes, he has created the so-called pizza diagrams, in which factions are represented as different slices of pizza pulled apart from the center, where the "work" (often difficult to articulate at first) of a given adaptive challenge tends to reside.
2. *Managing Disequilibrium.* A common metaphor for creating a productive range of disturbance in a given system is that of heat. To manage disequilibrium is to keep the "temperature" of a given situation in a productive zone of heat. For example, one might raise a touchy issue at a meeting, such as whether the administration of a university will tolerate expressions of racism on campus. Feelings about such a charged issue might raise the "heat" in the room, and the discussion would need to be facilitated with skill in order for things not to get out of hand. To borrow another image used by Heifetz, this is similar to cooking a stew. If the flame is turned up too high, the food in the

pot burns; if it is too low, it rots from being under-cooked. Similarly, if a challenge is not attended to, it will rot the system; if it is attended to with too much intensity (or "heat"), people and institutions may boil over to the point of being unable to work or being unworkable, respectively.

3. *Parsing the Difference Between Technical Work and Adaptive Challenges.* This concept formulates the core of the adaptive leadership approach. While technical challenges are seen as appropriately fitting with a known "repertoire" of responses (Heifetz, 1994), adaptive challenges are murkier—both in their definitions and their solutions. A key mistake made by people unfamiliar with this approach is to substitute technical work as a "fix" for an adaptive challenge. Again, the example of test scores comes to mind. Because standardized tests are part of the known repertoire for assessing learning, when school systems appear to be failing, the technical solution is often to increase the number and rigor of the tests. A more adaptive approach might be to consider the value our society places on the teaching profession.

4. *Distributing Loss at a Rate the Group Can Tolerate.* It takes a particular skill to distribute loss as a leader. Exercising leadership entails disappointing people's expectations.

    Whether it is overseeing the closing of schools, implementing federal regulations on testing standards, or coping with a union head's disappointment during a contract negotiation, superintendents must recognize that they are distributing loss to one faction or another every time they make a change. It takes courage and a high level of self-awareness to embrace this challenge.

    One example of a leader distributing loss at an acutely difficult moment in American history occurred when New York City Mayor Rudolph Giuliani spoke at a press conference on September 11, 2001. Giuliani was asked by reporters whether he had any idea what the number of casualties might be, and he responded poetically: "Whatever the numbers are," he said, "they will be more than we can bear." In that moment, Giuliani exercised one of the most difficult and subtle forms of leadership—to speak about unfathomable loss in a way that people could handle (cf. Flower, 1995).

5. *Distinguishing Being on the Balcony From Getting on the Dance Floor.* To "get on the balcony" means to mentally, emotionally, or even physically get a more detached view of a situation. Just as someone watching a football game from the point of view of the camera in a blimp can discern patterns on the gridiron of a football field that are undetectable at the 50-yard line, that person who can detach from the immediate entanglements of an often fast-moving situation may obtain a perspective that is crucial for progress. The meaning of this phrase is most apparent when learning in a setting that uses case-in-point methods of teaching and learning. The participant who

holds back from engagement may also be making keen observations about the patterns "on the dance floor" (sometimes referred to as "on the court" [Erhard, Jensen, Zaffron, & Granger, 2012]), where the active engagement—often with a certain amount of disequilibrium, such as political campaigns or ongoing crises—occurs. Ideally, a practitioner of adaptive leadership is able to orchestrate their own dance between the two perspectives and arrive at a sense of how to move the group forward in doing so.

6. *Staying Alive.* A person who disturbs the given stasis (including any leader) may make others uncomfortable to the point of inviting scapegoating, marginalization, or worse (cf., Smith & Berg, 1987). The challenge of productive leadership is to "live to fight another day," crafting interventions that will encourage change, but not push people too far. Heifetz characterizes the exercise of true leadership as "walking the razor's edge."

7. *Orchestrating Conflict.* One of the key tenets of productive adaptive work holds that conflict is inevitable and may serve as a resource to be utilized rather than an obstacle to be overcome. It takes skill to discern the usefulness of a given conflict, it takes a keen sense of experience to expect its presence, and it takes artistry to orchestrate the "music" of conflict productively. Heifetz's example of Environmental Protection Agency (E.P.A.) Administrator William Ruckelshaus's productive dialogues with the citizens of Tacoma, Washington, around the potential shutdown of a health-hazardous industry serves as a clear example of orchestrating conflict (Heifetz, 1994). In terms of group dynamics or group relations, conflict is often orchestrated when an authority figure "gives the work back to the group"—i.e., eschews the role of being "the answer guy (or girl)" and encourages the group reliant upon him or her to come up with their own proposals or solutions.

8. *Listening for the Song Beneath the Words.* An often-used metaphor for discerning the values of a group is that of being able to discern its melody or tune. This concept is both mysterious and visceral. It is mysterious because multiple meanings can be drawn out of it. Just as "one person's meat may be another one's poison," one person's harmony may be another person's cacophony. To lead a group effectively, one must have the capacity to hear both. This notion is, when taught in the classroom, also visceral because of the "music exercise" that is often used to convey it (cf. Parks, 2005). For example, an emphasis on etymology accompanies the teaching of adaptive leadership, wherein students are asked to consider the histories contained in words that stand out in their discussions. Given that the word "lead" also contains the Indo-European root of *leit*—meaning, "to go forth, to die"—the image of the warrior and perhaps the music of battle is contained in that word. One might also hear the music of courage when reflecting on what it means to lead.

9. *Distinguishing Between Formal and Informal Authority.* Formal authority is the sort of authority that comes with a title and a distinct position within an organization or group. For example, the positions of CEO of a company, town mayor, or high school principal are all positions of formal authority. They come with a clear contract for service: providing direction, protection, and order (Heifetz, 1994).

Informal authority is arguably more difficult to achieve. It consists of what some have called the "soft power" of influence or attraction to one's cause (cf., Nye, 2004; Snook, 2004). Informal authority is what politicians strive to attain before winning office, as they gather followers and make interventions into the public discourse. A contemporary example of someone who holds informal authority in popular culture is singer Beyoncé Knowles, whose politically tinged performance at the 50th American Super Bowl caused widespread controversy, as did the release of her music video "Formation" the day before. The controversy and public conversation that ensued were measures of the singer and pop icon's informal authority. Within two days of the release of "Formation," it had been downloaded seven million times—an additional measure of informal authority.

Another way of measuring informal authority is via political polling, wherein the popularity of an authority figure is discerned at the grassroots level. Those leaders who hold formal authority and exercise leadership most successfully are those who have managed to earn informal authority as well.

These concepts and definitions formed the core learning of the superintendents who participated in PLS. While it is in no way proposed here that their individual professional and learning journeys form a representative sample of all superintendents, the themes that have emerged from their individual and collective narratives are consistent with research on trends in education policies and their attendant dilemmas. From my own interpretive lens, to borrow a metaphor from the natural sciences, the limited scope of the superintendents' stories is similar to the miniature size of the ferns that together comprise the larger leafy plant—smaller parts that show a macro view of the whole. A story that is passed around the proverbial water cooler or village square is a fractal of the larger society's narrative (Snowden, 2012). What follows is a series of what I might tentatively call fractals—stories of urban school superintendents and their struggles that represent the larger whole of the public education system in the US.

Note

1. When referring to "empirically," I refer to Schwandt (2001), who makes the distinction amongst various definitions of empirical research. I do not propose

that this study was strictly empirical; rather, my research is a product of the "interpretive turn in the human sciences" (Schwandt, 2001, p. 68). This turn, as Schwandt asserts, "is marked by the belief that all knowledge claims are interpretations, and that there is nothing to appeal to in judging an interpretation but other interpretations" (Schwandt, 2001, pp. 68–69).

References

Bennis, W. (1959). Leadership theory and administrative behavior. *Administrative Science Quarterly, 4*, 259–301.

Bion, W. R. (1961). *Experiences in groups and other papers.* London: Tavistock Publications.

Erhard, W., Jensen, M. C., Zaffron, S., & Granger, K. L. (2012). *Creating leaders: An ontological/phenomenological model.* Working Paper. Harvard Business School Negotiations, Organizations and Markets Unit Research Paper Series No. 11-037; Barbados Group Working Paper No. 10-10; Simon School Working Paper No. FR-10-30; Retrieved from Social Sciences Research Network website: http://ssrn.com/abstract=1681682.

Flower, J. (1995). A conversation with Ronald Heifetz: Leadership without easy answers. *The Healthcare Forum Journal, 38*(4). Retrieved from: http://www.well.com/~bbear/heifetz.html.

Guilleux, F. (2011). *A developmental perspective on leadership education of aspiring principals.* Doctoral dissertation. Retrieved from ProQuest Dissertations and Theses database (UMI No. 3471901).

Heifetz, R. (1994). *Leadership without easy answers.* Cambridge, MA: Harvard University Press.

Heifetz, R., Grashow, A., & Linsky, M. (2009). *The practice of adaptive leadership: Tools and tactics for changing your organization and the world.* Cambridge, MA: Harvard Business School Press.

Heifetz, R., & Laurie, D. (1997). The work of leadership. *Harvard Business Review, 75*(1), 124–134.

Heifetz, R., & Linsky, M. (2004). When leadership spells danger. *Educational Leadership, 61*(7), 33–37.

Heifetz, R., & Sinder, R. (1991a). Teaching and assessing leadership courses: Part one. *National Forum, 71*(1), 21.

Heifetz, R., & Sinder, R. (1991b). Teaching and assessing leadership courses: Part two. *National Forum, 71*(2), 36.

Holton, E. F., & Baldwin, T. T. (Eds.). (2003). Making transfer happen: An action perspective on learning transfer systems. In E. F. Holton & T. T. Baldwin (Eds.), *Improving learning transfer in organizations.* San Francisco, CA: Jossey Bass.

Lemann, N. (2001, July 2). Testing limits. *New Yorker*, 28–34.

Mezirow, J., & Associates. (2000). *Learning as transformation: Critical perspectives on a theory in progress.* San Francisco, CA: Jossey Bass.

Nye, J. (2004). *Soft power: The means to succeed in world politics.* New York: Public Affairs.

O'Brien, T. J. (2016). *Looking for development in leadership development: Impacts of experiential and constructivist methods on graduate students and graduate schools.* Doctoral dissertation. Retrieved from Harvard University Digital Access to Scholarship at Harvard: https://dash.harvard.edu/handle/1/27112706

Parks, S. D. (2005). *Leadership can be taught: A bold approach for a complex world.* Boston, MA: Harvard Business School Press.

Rost, J. C. (1991). *Leadership for the twenty-first century.* New York, NY: Praeger Publishers.
Schwandt, T. A. (2001). *Dictionary of qualitative inquiry.* Thousand Oaks, CA: Sage Publications.
Smith, K., & Berg, D. (1987). *Paradoxes in group life.* San Francisco, CA: Jossey Bass.
Snook, S. (2004). Be, know, do: Forming character the West Point way. *Compass: A Journal of Leadership, 1*(2), 16–19.
Snowden, D. (2012, October 22). Combining complexity theory with narrative research. Ohio State Wexner Medical Center. Retrieved from: https://www.youtube.com/watch?v=pHjeFFGug1Y&t=12s.
Tschannen-Moran, M. (2014). *Trust matters: Leadership for successful schools.* San Francisco, CA: Jossey Bass.
Williams, D. (2005). *Real leadership.* San Francisco: Berrett-Koehler.

2 Participating Superintendents
Profiles in Leadership—and Survival

The stories of each of the superintendents I interviewed contain representative challenges that are woven into the fabric of our society. In order to give the reader a sense of their voices, I have largely quoted them without comment, although their interpretations of their situations are subjective. For example, all three of the superintendents who identified as Caucasian discussed racial issues in their districts as being highly charged.

Although eight superintendents comprised my original study, I have chosen only to discuss in detail the professional life histories that five of them shared. It is my belief that, taken together, their challenges are symptomatic of the challenges of top administrators in this complex national educational system of ours. Indeed, the very reluctance of these administrators to have their data shared beyond the immediate confines of the more circumscribed research project upon which this book is based is indicative of the protective boundaries urban school superintendents feel they must draw around themselves as they contend with the fact that they are often targets of public animosity or, at the very least, frustrations with the system.

The interviews upon which these portraits are based took place approximately six years after the conclusion of their participation in the PLS. While this might be seen as a disadvantage in terms of the freshness of their recollections, it is reasonable to suggest that there can be distinct advantages to asking people to recall their experiences years after the event because the "stickiness" (cf. Gladwell, 2002)—another term might be, the sustainable applicability—of the experience will come through. For my part, I was struck by the vividness and the positive feelings with which the superintendents recollected their experiences of the program.

Untangling Complexity

In a well-known passage from her seminal psychological novel *Middlemarch*, the great Victorian writer George Eliot describes the scratches on a pier-glass mirror as "events," and the illuminating candle, reflected in those scratches, as casting the illusion of those scratches coming into a kind of order. In Eliot's view, the candle is a metaphor for the individual ego, that part of the psyche which has a tendency to perceive random events as having a kind of order, an order which affects only itself.

> Your pier-glass or extensive surface of polished steel, made to be rubbed by a house-maid, will be minutely and multitudinously scratched in all directions; but place now against it a lighted candle as a centre of illumination and lo! The scratches will seem to arrange themselves in a fine series of concentric circles round that little sun. It is demonstrable that the scratches are going everywhere impartially, and it is only your candle which produces the flattering illusion of a concentric arrangement, its light falling within an exclusive optical selection. These things are a parable. The scratches are events, and the candle is the egoism of any person now absent.
> (Eliot, 1930, p. 310)

The passage in *Middlemarch* provides a kind of parable-as-filter for the enormity of societal problems. In the former, the human condition is presented as an interpretation of actions from the point of view of an individual "egoism," what might today be called a kind of narcissism. And while Eliot depreciates the candle that forms concentric circles out of random events as the folly of "egoism," here I am appropriating Eliot's metaphor into a more positive kind of framing. The metaphor of Eliot's candle in terms of my own narrative serves as the point of view of an individual within a confused situation, an organizing principle of illumination that clarifies the surround of events so that we can make better sense of them. Such are the superintendents of PLS: points of light whose stories illuminate the often-chaotic situation of urban education in America.

Each of the superintendent portraits that follows is a portrait of endurance, because the political complexities of any urban system in this country are attended by myriad challenges, all of which rise and fall within the context of the larger systems within which a superintendent operates. Each of these superintendents' stories sheds light on the complexity of urban public education in America.

What follows are five portraits of survival—or, perhaps better put, efforts at survival—within the urban school superintendency. Just over half of the superintendents were male. Three identified as Caucasian, two as non-white. Two of them left the districts of which they were in charge "under a cloud"—resignations that were more or less forced upon them by circumstances—and three of them moved on of their own accord. Tables 2.1 and 2.2 outline their own and that of their respective districts' demographics.

Table 2.1 Demographic Distribution of Sample

Superintendent's Pseudonym	Ethnicity	Gender	Age at Time of Participation in PLS	Location of District During PLS
John Brown {cloud}	Caucasian	M	50s	Northeast
Bobby Harris	African American	M	60s	Pacific Northwest
Dee Rowe	Caucasian	F	50s	Midwest
Tom Swain {cloud}	Caucasian	M	60s	Tri-State Area
Maria Torres	Latina	F	50s	Tri-State Area

Table 2.2 Student Demographic Information for Superintendents' Districts

Superintendent	District	Percentage of Children on Free/Reduced Lunch	Percentage of Student Population Comprising Children of Color
Maria Torres	Northeastern US	53%	95%
Bobby Harris	Northwestern US	25.8%	16.5%
Tom Swain	East Coast, US	Not Available	49.5%
Dee Rowe	Midwest US	62%	41.35%
John Brown	Northeastern US	71.2%	78.2%

Demographic Information on the Districts

Within these profiles, I offer some demographic sketches of the districts in which each of these superintendents served at the time of his or her participation in PLS.

Table 2.2 captures student demographic information—obtained through the PLS superintendents' district offices—of the superintendents' districts, during the time they attended PLS (2002–2003). To protect confidentiality, sources are not listed for this information.

Five Portraits

John Brown

John Brown is a tall, soft-spoken man with a penchant for discussing intellectual ideas and a palpable desire to connect to others. He was born in 1951 in a Northeastern city in the Tri-State area. He is married with no children. In 1977, he received his doctorate in education and was certified as a school administrator through the Southeastern state where he was based for much of his career. For the duration of PLS, he was managing a turbulent, low-income district in the industrial Northeast with a large immigrant population. His story is one of attempting to manage factions around issues of race. As a Caucasian male, he perceived himself at a political disadvantage in managing the district of which he was in charge, the one he was managing when he participated in PLS, District S.

During the time he participated in PLS, John was serving in this, his first superintendency. District S.'s poverty index is reflected in the fact that close to 80% of the public school students in the district received free or reduced lunch during his tenure. During John's tenure, the dropout rate in District S. was at nearly 50%. As is often the case with situations of limited resources, the politics of the community were fierce, and this ultimately led to John's resignation after serving as superintendent from 2001 until 2008.

Another dynamic at play was that of race. Thus, the tension of competition for financial resources, coupled with those that ensued from race issues in the district (a population mainly comprised of people of color guided by a Caucasian white male as the top authority figure, the students in District S. were taught by a largely white population of teachers) led to John's being pushed out.

John's PLS Case

Arriving in 2001 as a superintendent of this high-needs district, John was embroiled in the politics of unions and city politicians. In an effort to turn around the district, he created a city-wide "branding" of the district for the teachers, parents, and students to embrace, an effort which foundered on the hard realities of bankruptcy and sanctions by federal agencies for failing schools. Because of the financial woes of the city, the financial control board put in place by the state ultimately trumped the desires of the local control board. By the time of his departure, John said that the financial control board had "some new agendas, and one of them was that they wanted a new superintendent, and clearly the agenda was that they wanted a . . . superintendent [who was a person of color]." While recollecting this episode in an interview with me, John said, "I understood that [desire for a person of color to run the district]." Indeed, John's successor was an African American former military officer who moved across the country to take the job in District S.

It should be noted that John was a candidate and a finalist for several other jobs during his tenure in District S. Since his departure in 2008, he has served in the department of education of another state, and as district superintendent of two other somewhat smaller districts in a Southeastern state. At the time of my interview with him, he was about to leave his third superintendency.

Throughout his interview, John appeared to be very candid when discussing the work of balancing the needs of different factions, and appreciative of the lessons from PLS about superintendents being cognizant of the personal toll this kind of work would take. "Quite frankly," he said,

> That's something that wears on you after a while, that's something [the main instructor for PLS] was pushing on. People have different needs, different sets of comfort levels. How do you get to be in the "stew" and get [these factions] to be content with the greater good for the whole community?

John's Post-PLS Case

At the time of his interview with me, John was serving as a superintendent of a small Southeastern county, County K., where he had been for approximately 17 months. Here also he alluded to multiple fiscal issues with which he had to contend. A recent accomplishment he cited was the successful negotiation of a teacher's contract that included performance pay. The current challenge he faced was how to develop and implement an International Baccalaureate program throughout the district. He also spoke of how to implement the state's Race to the Top proposal, an Obama Administration initiative, which rewarded innovation in teaching in K–12 education and involved funding from the federal government's education department (Civic Impulse, 2018).

What the Cases Had in Common

In both of John's cases, the case of District S. and the case of County K., the theme of managing disequilibrium emerged sharply. The difference between the two had to do with the fact that in District S. the disequilibrium was high and needed to be tamped down, while in County K. John perceived that it would be best to turn the heat up so as to "cook the stew" better. In terms of survival, the arc of John's tenure in District S. is complete. Here he seemed to find it the better part of valor to leave District S. without becoming a "lightning rod" for a split community in which one faction wanted him to stay (the local school board) and another wanted him to leave (the financial control board). In his own words, he said,

> I had to make a choice of whether to ask those board members to go to court [and fight the state-imposed financial control board] and continue to fight it and split the community or not. And it seemed to me that it was not going to be helpful, given the overall direction that we were trying to move the system [of District S.] . . . to then continue to go into court, fight that battle, and split the community and create all of that division. And I just decided not to do that. And

I think for me personally I tend to be more of a unifier, I tend to come from the perspective of, Things work better when you pull people together rather than you push people apart. So I don't like being a polarizing leader in that respect, I don't like the notion of being a lightning rod for dividing the community. That's just not a role that I really like. So I'd much rather just try and bring people together and create unity of purpose rather than divisions.

Here John evinced his philosophy and temperament as someone who sought to unify rather than divide, and as someone who was very likely averse to conflict in most cases. Yet as other portions of my interview with him will show, he was also someone who could be prone to frustration when he sensed that the heat in the system was not high enough.

Bobby Harris

Bobby presents as a low-key, gentle person of seriousness. Often during the large group discussions in PLS, he would appear silent yet wholly attentive. When he spoke, others listened. He was born in 1944 in a small city in a mid-Atlantic state. He is divorced and the father of one child. He holds graduate degrees in social psychology as well as in public administration and education policy administration. In 1999, he was certified as a school administrator. In addition to PLS, Bobby also participated in several other leadership training programs. He has not taught school at any level. Prior to becoming a superintendent, he served as director of human resources for the central office in his district and as assistant superintendent in a West Coast city. Over 20 years of Bobby's experience has been in the field of human resources.

Bobby had served as superintendent of his district in the Pacific Northwest, District 4, for 12 years: 1999–2011. He described his district as "progressive" and "similar to Cambridge, Massachusetts" in that it is a university town where the professed values of many of the professionals are liberal and political party affiliation was mostly Democratic. At the time of his participation in PLS, 25.8% of the children in Bobby's district were on free or reduced lunch, and 16.5% were children of color. According to Bobby, the liberal values held by much of the population in his district did not extend to the distribution of equity to underserved children, who were not given the same access to more selective public schools as those children from families of greater privilege. These values were thrown into greater relief under the mandate of budget cuts.

Bobby's PLS Case

The case that Bobby recalled during his interview with me focused on an incident that occurred at the tail end of the PLS program, in 2004, when a faction representing an ethnic minority in the community sought to name one of the schools in the district after a minority community's civil rights hero, while the school board wanted to name the school after a form of local wildlife.

This case, like so many of the cases from PLS, while it centered on a particular issue at a particular time, represented much larger societal forces that were swirling through the district. Thus while Bobby discussed the larger (arguably more amorphous) issue of middle-class and upper-middle-class families being unwilling to "walk the talk" of their values of equity, the particular challenges that informed the case of naming the school were more precise expressions of these larger forces. When a board member objected to naming the new school for a minority group's civil rights hero, this was an expression of the phenomenon social scientists refer to as NIMBY (Not In My Back Yard)—meaning, that while we may embrace the aspirations of equity in the abstract, when the concrete reality of equity edges closer to home—i.e., "my backyard"—we resist. For example, two professional parents may "support" or "believe in" the principle of free education for all, and the notion of children from upper-middle-class homes attending school alongside children who are homeless, the uncomfortable consequences of overcrowded, under-resourced public schools may quickly become intolerable for such parents, and they may make the decision to opt for private schools, or move to a better neighborhood, where the tax base supports more desirable public schools. "There was," Bobby recalled,

> One [school] board member who was adamant that we shouldn't be naming [the school] to serve one particular part of the community, and that it was a community school and not just the Latino community school and so forth and so on. In this case, as opposed to John's, Bobby was able to prevail, and his job remained intact.

After consulting with other members of PLS on the conflict in his district over this particular issue, he was able to persuade his board members that the minority Latino community's desire to have a new school bear the name of a social justice advocate from the 1960s had merit. After partnering with a couple of the board members to explain why the name was as important as it was, and after inviting representatives from the National Association for the Advancement of Colored People (NAACP), the American Civil Liberties Union (ACLU) ACLU, and a community organization—as well as from the local branch of a Latina/o organization—the board voted 6–1 to support the name change in favor of the civil rights hero.

Bobby's Post-PLS Case

The case Bobby described related to working with stakeholder values. During his interview, he spoke of a critical incident involving the merging of schools and how he worked with competing factions to forge a compromise that provided a more equitable distribution of resources to the community without overriding the values of a certain faction of the community. This case took place several years after the "naming" controversy. In this case, the issue was again a byproduct of the merging of schools in order to cope with budgetary shortfalls and create efficiency. In this case, the faction objecting to the merging was largely from the Jewish community in Bobby's district. The school that was going to be closed was a "choice" school that was, according to Bobby, "a kind of mainstay in the Jewish community to which mostly Jewish families sent their kids." It was also a school that lacked economic diversity, with a higher proportion of upper-bracket SES students than not, as well as far fewer children with special education needs. Bobby recalled:

> I had recommended closing it and I had gone out and met with the parents and the staff and they had tried to talk me out of closing it. I was very clear about why. Then we got into negotiating . . . and they had said, So if you're going to close us and if we're going to have to consolidate, Can we do this? Can we do that? And my response was, Well, I'm not sure anything's closed off, but we can't continue to have this building and this school into the future.

The upshot was that the group of people represented by two of the teachers who had wanted to maintain the choice school approached Bobby with the idea of merging with another school slated for shutdown, one with a higher proportion of students of color, students in lower income brackets, and students with special needs. As Bobby recalled,

> So I said to the folks, OK, here's what you do. You guys put a small committee together, come up with how you would see this working, and I'll meet with you after you've got an original plan. I'm not saying that I'll support it, but if it looks like it has possibilities and you can meet the goals that the board has set—that it will be a diverse school, [and] that it will be open and it will serve the neighborhood kids as well, not just all kids who want to come based on choice—then I'll at least be willing to entertain taking it to the board and seeing if they will reverse the decision.

After six weeks, the group came up with the proposal for an experimental merging of the two schools, and the board allowed them to have a provisional existence for a year. Since then, the new school has been declared a success by the board, "And now," said Bobby, "they're a thriving school."

What the Cases Had in Common

Both of these cases emerged from the nationwide pressure on districts to streamline school operations in order to make them more efficient. This pressure has emerged from the business mindset that has overtaken the educational system in America (cf., Crawford-Garrett, n.d.). Yet budgetary pressures are quite real, and Bobby was not hostile to taking them on. He spoke extensively in his interview about the usefulness of professional development that would address these fiscal realities. At the time of his interview, Bobby underscored the issue of budgetary pressures on his district at this moment in time, which were worse than any he had ever seen before. (It should be noted that Bobby's interview with me took place a couple of years after the global financial meltdown of 2008.)

Dee Rowe

Dee is an outgoing, athletic woman whose appreciation for others exudes a down-to-earth quality. She is a Caucasian female born in the Midwest in 1950. She is married and has no children. She has spent her entire life in the mid-sized Midwestern city where she was born. In 1987, she was certified through the university at which she earned her master's degree. She holds a Ph.D. in education leadership. For seven years, she was a teacher at the elementary school level. She served for five years as a deputy superintendent in the district of the city where she grew up and succeeded her supervisor as superintendent from 2002 to 2007. At the time of her participation in PLS, 62% of children in her district were on free or reduced lunch and 41.35% of students were children of color. The superintendency she held at the time of her participation in PLS was her first and only superintendency. In 2007, she left the superintendency to serve in her current position: executive director of an education advocacy group for large urban districts, the job she held at the time of her interview with me.

Dee spent the bulk of her interview discussing the value of PLS, and how important it was for her to be exposed to the ideas of adaptive leadership early on in her first superintendency. Participating in the program, she said, was "literally life-changing." She also spoke extensively about how important it was for her to work with her faculty consultant, Larry (a teaching faculty in PLS who visited Dee between sessions of the executive training program), whom she hired as a consultant following the termination of PLS. The case she discussed in the greatest detail took place after PLS and had to do with the dilemma of hiring a principal who was the best fit for a high-needs high school in her district.

Dee's Post-PLS Case

The case that emerged from Dee's interview centered around the decision process she undertook in hiring a what she perceived as a more qualified white female over a less-qualified yet more charismatic African American male for a principal position at a lower performing middle school in her district. It was clear to her that there were factional divisions in the community around this critical decision. In her district, she said,

> We always used a collaborative process for that [kind of hiring decision] and a representative process. So when we got finished doing the initial round of interviews there was a real division about what the person in the community wanted and the person that the school folks wanted. And it was the difference of a white female candidate who had a lot of the academic background and experience and had certainly worked in schools in that neighborhood . . . versus a young African American man who was very good with the community piece and who was popular with folks and was just real congenial and charismatic. And it was going to be a dilemma because he was a great guy, but he didn't have the depth of knowledge to be able to lead the academic piece of that [i.e., the school]. If you could put the two together, it would be . . . the perfect candidate.

After deciding to hire the white female candidate because of what she perceived as the greater needs of the school for which she was hiring, Dee took the step of enlisting someone from the local chapter of the NAACP to talk to the black male candidate to explain why he would be passed over for the job. She asked this person to go to coffee, a tactic suggested frequently in the teaching of adaptive leadership for how to partner with an opposing faction.

> I . . . explained to him what I was doing and why I was doing it. And [that] it was really out of my care and concern for the school that I really thought the white female was the better candidate for that position. And, again, the opportunities that I wanted to give this other gentleman to be able to prepare him to take a position like this in the future. . . . Anyway, long story short, it was one of those things that was the right thing to do. Because he [the local leader of the local NAACP chapter] very much appreciated hearing from me on the front end. And I think it helped defuse what might have become a more dramatic situation.

Here, Dee is also demonstrating the principle of keeping disequilibrium within the range of productivity—in this case, by partnering strategically with a faction that stood to sustain some loss.

Tom Swain: "The Shadow of Heifetz Has Passed Through"

Tom is an obviously intellectual yet down to earth and humorous man whose penchant for self-revealingly honest remarks is disarming. A Caucasian male born in 1940 in a Northeastern city, he is married and has two children. He holds a doctorate in educational administration. In 1971, he was certified as a school administrator through the department of education at an East Coast research university. He served in multiple roles as a central office administrator and was a teacher for two years at the high school level. He served as an urban school superintendent in only one city before moving into academia as a full-time professor of practice in education.

At the time of his interview with me, Tom was working as a professor of practice in the education school of a prestigious research university located on the East Coast. He had held this position for five years, following his resignation from the superintendency in a large industrial urban district of a neighboring state.

Tom served in his one urban school superintendency for eight years: 1998–2006. Multiple attempts to retrieve student demographic data from this district during the time of Tom's participation in PLS were fruitless, and repeated phone calls to his district were not returned. A survey conducted of the district in 2010—approximately eight years after Tom's participation in PLS—showed a poverty index of 25% of students receiving free and reduced lunches in the schools. Tom's resignation from the superintendency was the result of increasingly contentious relations with his board, which was, in his words, "lining up to shoot me."

Tom's Cases: PLS and Post-PLS

Tom came to PLS with a fair amount of sophistication regarding group dynamics and leadership work. Much of the language he used during his interview, as he reflected on PLS, also seemed to indicate that he was familiar with psychotherapy. He was one of the few individuals in the group of participants who spoke about the fact that one of the main teachers of PLS had been trained as a psychiatrist. He said that he felt that the superintendent's role was, in part, to generate conflict. He described himself as "not particularly conservative, and not risk-averse." At the same time, he framed the overall challenge in his district in terms of the fact that he had only so much political capital to spend when he arrived in the district, capital he chose to spend by making a number of changes by relocating or dismissing some school principals (all of whom happened to be African American). He seemed keenly aware that his ethnicity was going to be a factor in his leadership. Tom was the first white person in 25 years to serve as superintendent in this largely black East Coast urban district.

At the beginning of his interview, Tom focused on the fact that his resignation was more or less forced. Prior to his resignation, a new African American male board member had had Tom investigated for financial corruption, although the investigation found no wrongdoing on Tom's part. Tom spoke ruefully of the fact that, of the three African American women he had tried to groom for succession, none was interviewed for the position by the school board. He felt that conflict with his school board was a central factor in his superintendency, and he resigned a year before his contract was up for renewal in order to take a teaching position at a nearby research university. He described the person the board chose as his successor as a "yes-person" to the board.

During Tom's tenure as superintendent of his district, he sent one of his principals, one who had been struggling to lead her school, to an intensive experiential training in leadership at the Center for Creative Leadership in North Carolina, a program he likened to PLS's teaching of adaptive leadership via case-in-point methods. He also referred to his published articles and book chapters on the work of teaching of adaptive leadership in PLS, and its value to him both personally and professionally. In his graduate courses at the university where he teaches, he uses Heifetz and Linsky's *Leadership on the Line* (2002) as a text. "So the shadow of Heifetz has passed through."

He also described a case that involved one of his deputies, one with whom he continually came into conflict but felt he could not fire because of the fact that Tom was white, and his deputy was black. This case had come up for discussion during his participation in PLS as well as when he reflected on the learning since his participation in the program. The following excerpt from my interview with Tom describes the heightening tensions with his deputy:

> I think he hoped he would be superintendent before I came but was not considered by the then-board as the right candidate. . . . He was very conservative, very risk-averse, and here's me—[someone] who is not particularly conservative and not risk-averse. So I'm really pushing things, and a lot of the push is a little problematic for him. And I also knew, and know about myself, that I need people near me that need to pull things back; there needs to be some kind of reality orientation or some conservatism. So I'm not afraid to have some very strong and opinionated people near me. Certainly, in terms of the business manager, chief financial officer for the district, I recruited, selected, and appointed somebody who was extremely independent and was not afraid to tell me I was wrong and so on, but was also phenomenal at the job he did. But there were times when I thought that the deputy superintendent was really holding things back. And there were occasions when I thought that he was sort of double-dealing . . . he'd make a commitment to do X and he'd do Y behind

my back. And we had a couple of shoot-outs. I rarely get angry with people, and once or twice in cabinet meetings, he and I *really* got into it, which is pretty unusual for me.

Tom never fired the deputy, however, and felt that he was forced out of his position at the end of his tenure as superintendent.

Maria Torres

Born in 1949, Maria Torres is a woman of Hispanic origin, who grew up in a large urban community in the Northeastern US. She is divorced and has one son. She holds master's degrees in psychology and in educational administration and was certified by the State Education Department of a Northeastern state in the US (where she also grew up) in 1978. In addition to PLS, she listed three other leadership training programs in which she participated: the Institute for Educational Leadership in Washington, DC; the Center for Educational Leadership; and the Institute for Learning.

Maria's experience as an educator included seven years as a teacher at the elementary level, three years as an executive assistant to an urban superintendent, and three years as an urban deputy superintendent. Prior to retiring from the urban Northeastern district in which she last served as a regional superintendent, Maria was a district superintendent in one of the largest urban areas of the Northeastern US for nine years, from 1994 to 2003. At the time of Maria's participation in PLS, her district comprised both affluent and underserved children, 53% of whom were on free and reduced lunch and 95% of whom were children of color. A new mayor was elected in her city during her tenure, and shortly thereafter, a new chancellor was appointed to restructure the sprawling school system that included Maria's district.

During her participation in PLS, Maria presented a case on the difficulty of creating a new school that would attract the affluent while remaining equally open to the underserved children of her district. During the two years in which she participated in PLS, she witnessed and engaged in a massive restructuring of the Northeastern city where her district was located. She was later given the responsibility of overseeing two of the merged restructured districts. After retiring in 2006, Maria continued to work in the city's department of education, focusing on issues of literacy. At the time of her interview with me, Maria was serving in a consulting position to support collaborative efforts to improve teaching in the same urban area in which she served as a superintendent during the time of PLS.

Two distinct cases emerged during my interview with Maria. The first concerned establishing a new school in the district for which she served as superintendent from 1994 until 2003. The second case concerned the massive restructuring of the education system and her role as an authority figure.

Maria's PLS Case 1

Maria described an episode that took place at her district when she began attending PLS. She was creating a new school in a district of diverse socioeconomic status when a conflict arose between two factions in the community: one, a more affluent one with stakeholders who wanted to maintain a certain caliber of education, and another, less affluent faction, whose stakeholders wanted access to better schools. It was clear that the more affluent faction was fearful that children from a lower socioeconomic status would diminish the caliber of education in their schools. One faction of the community voiced concern that minority students in a certain zone would not have the opportunity to attend this school. Maria spoke of the difficulty in balancing the needs of competing factions and coming up with a compromise by creating a lottery system for seats in the more desirable school. The resolution to the problem, however, remained a political hot potato.

> And so it became really a very difficult [problem] for us as an administration. Eventually, we agreed on two middle school/high schools. And while the percentage of minority students in the [affluent part of the community's] school did decrease, it wasn't . . . very significant. . . . And [so] we agreed on a lottery program where students from both [affluent and underserved population] zones could actually—if they wanted to—could be considered through a lottery for seat, set aside some seats. . . . So it became a real big hot spot.

Maria's PLS Case 2

The second case Maria described involved a city-wide restructuring of the education department in the municipality that contained her district. During this time—one in which a number of educators in the city lost their jobs—Maria was given greater responsibilities and became superintendent of two districts comprising a "region." A consistent theme to emerge from this case had to do with managing the pain of others as they went through the process of enormous change. Reflecting on this episode, Maria spoke about "a lot of unknowns and [how] people were anxious." At the time she saw herself as needing to support people through this change and contain their anxiety. She spoke at length about the empathy she felt for her colleagues during the restructuring process taking place in the city, and at the same time of the necessity for supporting this change, as she became a part of the new authority structure. She said, "People felt the turmoil and the changes . . . and you needed to sort of help them understand the reasons why. Why the goal was to support schools in a better—how we did need to restructure ourselves."

What the Cases Had in Common

Both of Maria's cases involved the challenges presented by change. As has often been stated, "people don't fear change, they fear loss" (cf. Heifetz, 1994). While this observation could be applied to numerous dilemmas that the superintendents in this study faced, it seems particularly applicable to Maria's descriptions of her experiences. In both cases, momentous change was coming to a community. In the first of her two cases, the change was arriving in a community that was accustomed to school choice. People feared the loss of what they could expect from their local public school. In the second case, change arrived in a sector that employed many thousands of people and had done so for decades, and people feared the loss of their livelihood. Moving things forward without losing her own authority meant "walking a tightrope," as Maria described it later.

Influence of Context on Application of Adaptive Leadership Learning: A Brief Analysis

This section describes certain aspects of the superintendents' contexts discussed during their interviews, and the positive or negative influence these contexts had upon the application of their learning *in situ*. The discussion also examines how adaptive leadership concepts learned in PLS affected superintendents' understanding of their situations.

Four categories emerged from the interviews as distinct contexts for the superintendents' learning: 1) school boards, 2) politics, 3) external mandates, and 4) structural/systemic changes. The frequency with which these topics arose is shown in Table 2.3. Four areas of context emerged as affected by superintendents' learnings: 1) getting to the balcony on the overall gestalt of the job, 2) interactions with school boards,

Table 2.3 Findings for Superintendents' Contexts

Suptdt.	School Boards	Politics	Instructional Core	External Mandates	Structural/ Systemic Changes
Maria	X	X	X	X	X
Bobby		X			
Tom	X	X			X
Dee	X		X	X	
John	X	X			

26 Participating Superintendents

3) engagement with the community, and 4) politics (generally not in the sense of running for public office but rather in local issues).

The most frequently mentioned challenge for superintendents was that of school boards. The findings for context indicate that for four of the five superintendents, school boards and how to contend with them was the most frequently mentioned problematic reality. Of the five, Bobby was the only superintendent who did not describe his board as problematic. In the focus group interview, he was the only superintendent who tempered his description of school boards as "challenging" (rather than "evil"—one superintendent's term—or sub-optimal in their usefulness).

The second most frequently mentioned aspect of context was the general political climate, whether connected with national politics (as was the case with Dee) or local politics, or the politics of the community within their districts. Four of the five superintendents spoke of politics in a general way and, although national politics were at times alluded to, the notion of politics was largely discussed in the sense of group dynamics around a given issue (for example, Tom's reluctance to fire a black deputy due to what he was sure would be political fallout).

The third, fourth, and fifth categories—those that were least frequently mentioned as elements of the superintendents' context—were as follows. Third: What Elmore (2000) calls the "instructional core"; fourth: the external mandates, such as No Child Left Behind; and fifth: the structural/systemic changes taking place within a district (Maria's) and in the education landscape at large (Tom).

Of the five, two participants mentioned the instructional core as an important part of the contextual landscape for them. Maria spent a greater portion of her interview focusing on this aspect of running a district than did Diane and Sam. This may have been due to the fact that, although she had moved on from the superintendency at the time of her interview, she was serving in a leadership position for a literacy initiative in a large and complex urban district.

One theme that surfaced but was never articulated as an important "undiscussable" or "hidden issue" was the fact that superintendents earn salaries many times those of their teachers and, in fact, many public officials. In terms of adaptive leadership diagnoses, such hidden issues as these were poisoning the well of contentious conflict in these districts. Symptomatic of the tensions of this hidden issue is a 2014 episode for *This American Life* in which a reporter followed the conflicts of a suburban town in New York where a faction of Hasidim Jews who educated their children at private Yeshiva schools gained control of the school board, thus giving them control of how money was spent for the district. The ensuing budgetary cuts to the public schools, and the consequent arguments that arose between the faction of the religious minority group that controlled the school board and the more traditional population that lived in the town were striking for their vitriol. Eventually, the state stepped in to take control (Calhoun, 2014).

The fact that money is a source of power for superintendents with budgetary experience is also a source of the aggression toward them. As one of the superintendents once remarked, "There is an old African proverb that goes, the higher you climb, the more they can see of your behind." While somewhat crudely put, the general meaning here could be interpreted as the higher one climbs in status, the more exposure one can expect—especially, it would seem, of those who go into public service. Yet in multiple sessions with these superintendents over the course of two years, the issue of their personal compensation, to my knowledge, never came up.

Since PLS's termination, the issue of inequity in American society has become increasingly acute. The microcosm of this inequity may be viewed in vast urban districts where the "worker bees," or teachers, are paid a fraction of the salary of their senior authority figures. For example, the average teacher salary in Atlanta, Georgia, is just over $53,000 while the salary of its superintendent was, with compensation for housing and other retirement benefits, $387,000. Thus, this urban school superintendent's salary is more than seven times that of the average teacher.

Conclusion

It is fitting to end this series of portraits with a comment regarding the hidden issue of money. Hidden issues recall darkness, and here George Eliot's metaphor persists. It is not possible, within the scope of this small book, to fully illuminate the complexity of issues that contribute to the challenges of education in this country. Inasmuch as the light cast by the "little sun" of someone's case will offer an articulation that presents a kind of order on "random events," still, there will be scratches on the surface of our education system that appear to go nowhere and make little sense. The purpose of PLS was to increase this group of superintendents' self-awareness. However much their self-awareness was enhanced, however, there were blind spots. In the following chapter, we will see how PLS was remembered as a program, and how the superintendents' self-perceptions grew.

References

Calhoun, B. (2014, September 12). A not-so-simple majority. *This American Life*. Podcast retrieved from https://www.thisamericanlife.org/534/a-not-so-simple-majority

Civic Impulse. (2018). *H.R. 1532-112th Congress: Race to the Top Act of 2011*. Retrieved from www.govtrack.us/congress/bills/112/hr1532.

Crawford-Garrett, K. (n.d.). Teach for America and the new Taylorism in public education. Retrieved from: https://www.academia.edu/12448211/Teach_for_America_Urban_Reform_and_the_New_Taylorism_in_Public_Education?auto=download

Eliot, G. (1930/1991). *Middlemarch* (p. 277). New York, NY: Alfred A. Knopf.
Elmore, R. F. (2000). *Building a new structure for school leadership*. Washington, DC: The Albert Shanker Institute.
Gladwell, M. (2002). *The tipping point: How little things can make a big difference*. Boston, MA: Back Bay Books.
Glass, I. (Producer). (2014, September 12). *A not-so-simple majority* [audio podcast]. Retrieved from www.thisamericanlife.org.
Heifetz, R. (1994). *Leadership without easy answers*. Cambridge, MA: Harvard University Press.
Heifetz, R., & Linsky, M. (2002). *Leadership on the line*. Cambridge, MA: Harvard Business School Press.

3 Description of the Program for Leading Superintendents (PLS)

During PLS, the constellation of personalities, historical events, national policy, and a teaching method that invited personal risk was unusual. At its most basic level, PLS provided a safe space, a nurturing environment, for 12 high-profile individuals from across the US who were operating under circumstances of enormous stress. Yet this safe space was not created by the facilitators alone. It was every one of the participants who agreed to safeguard one another's confidentiality and who supported each participant's story of learning through active, non-judgmental listening that created a container that fostered growth, otherwise known as a "holding environment" (cf. Heifetz, 1994; Winnicott, 1986). The general feeling in the room was "I've been there—and if I haven't, there but for the grace of God go I." With perhaps one exception, to one degree or another, each of the superintendents was being asked to act as a change agent to solve the problem of leading a complex school system. Thus, the pressures on each one of them were great.

PLS was established as a pilot executive education program for a group of 12 superintendents from throughout the US. It was in many ways the culmination of a single program officer's (whom I will here call Samantha) vision for leadership training for urban school superintendents—a vision that seemed to have emerged following her participation in an annual workshop for Chief State School Officers from each of the 50 states in the summer of 2000. During this workshop, Samantha was exposed to the teaching of adaptive leadership by Don Walsh (a pseudonym for the faculty member at M university, which later housed the program). Samantha returned to her foundation and initiated the idea of a leadership training program for urban school superintendents in states that the foundation had targeted for five-year grants of approximately $5 million each. In each state, an urban district superintendent was invited to apply for funding to attend on-site sessions at M university, a top-tier research university in the Northeastern region US.

Beginning in the spring of 2002, the superintendents began to assemble—first, at an introductory convocation and conference, and later more formally at the university site. In May of 2002, the original group of superintendents gathered for a five-day intensive executive training program in adaptive leadership. The superintendents hailed from virtually every region of the US: Pacific Northwest, Midwest, Southeast, Mid-Atlantic, and Northeast. (The only region not represented in the cohort was the Southwest.) Each of the superintendents was responsible for a complex urban district. During their first meeting, they experienced case-in-point learning, a pedagogical method that demands vulnerability and humility as a facilitator makes observations about dynamics at play in the room reflecting the concepts being taught. For example, if the topic were "hidden issues" in group dynamics the facilitator might point to the hidden issues inside the room in which the session is taking place (e.g., gender dynamics).

Following the initial five-day meeting of the original 12 superintendents, subsequent meetings took place approximately once a quarter. These sessions were comprised of two half-day sessions and one full-day session. Superintendent participants would typically arrive on a Friday morning in time for an early afternoon session and depart at lunchtime on Sunday. Following the initial convening in May of 2002, the sessions occurred in July 2002, November 2002, March 2003, and July 2003. Although the sessions continued well into 2004, the focus of this book is on the first five sessions of learning, later called "Program for Leading Superintendents, Phase I."

Each in-residence session was divided between interactive lectures by the main teacher-facilitators of the program and small-group work among clusters of superintendents. The purpose of the small groups was to give participating superintendents time to apply the concepts they had learned to the actual problems they were facing in their districts. Each superintendent was instructed to bring a case of his or her own choosing—the case was based on a challenge that was either recent and unresolved or ongoing. The superintendents were explicitly instructed to not bring in successful "war stories." For example, a superintendent might present a case to his or her small group on how to manage the politics of the district during a municipal restructuring process over which the superintendent had little control, and little opportunity to offer input. Teaching faculty and other staff from M university sat in on the small groups, occasionally intervening in the discussions. The purpose was to offer some, but not too much, guidance to the discussion, leaving most of the work of analysis up to the small-group members themselves. This kind of "toggling" between large-group and small-group discussions not only offered diverse teaching practices but also allowed for illustrations in real time of a key concept: that of "parallel process" (see below).

The Teaching of Adaptive Leadership

Adaptive leadership is often taught in what is called a case-in-point fashion. This means that if a dynamic is happening in the room of the learning environment, particularly if it is a dynamic that is related to the theory being taught, the participants have license to call it out. For example, if the instructor were describing the phenomenon of work avoidance, the tendency of a group to avoid its "real," or central, task, then a participant might point out how work avoidance was happening in the room at that moment. Thus, if a society's task is to address a widening gap of income inequality, a method of work avoidance might be for a legislative body to pass a tax bill providing a false boost to the economy instead of asking hard questions about the systemic inequities in the system that have brought about such inequalities. At the classroom level a group of learners might consider what a spike in standardized test scores might mean to a community in terms of offering a short-lived boost to the morale of an underserved population of students, instead of doing the hard work of examining the systemic forces that allowed children to be educated at a sub-par level. Another somewhat subtler aspect of case-in-point teaching manifests as the phenomenon of *parallel process*.

Parallel Process

"Parallel process" is a term that emanates from psychotherapy, particularly the psychotherapeutic process of group facilitation. The phrase is meant to capture the idea that a parallel process occurs between orders of hierarchy in related groups. For example, a group of supervisors might find themselves wrestling with the same issues as a group of supervisees (DeLucia-Waack & Fauth, 2004). Such an issue might be that of male dominance. While a group of psychiatrists-in-training might be jockeying for positions of authority among themselves, the supervising group might be jockeying similarly. In the teaching of adaptive leadership, a small teaching group that meets before and after the class (or "large group") of students convenes might embody a dynamic that is reflected in the classroom. In similar fashion, the dynamics among the participating superintendents, it has been hypothesized, were reflective of the dynamics in their districts. One superintendent, for example, confessed to being an orphan who never felt he had a fixed home. In his professional life, he had a difficult time staying in a district beyond a few years.

Similar to the notion of holding environment, a term that also originates in psychiatry, parallel process has been extended to describe the means by which a number of larger systems are mirrored in minute reflections of them. For example, the Israeli-Palestinian conflict—as complexly layered as that conflict is—might show up in a sailing camp for Israeli and Palestinian youths in petty arguments among different factions or cliques.

One way of looking at parallel process is as a kind of fractal, wherein the smaller group dynamic becomes a microcosm of what is happening in the larger group. The purpose, then, of each superintendent presenting a case on his or her district was twofold: First, it was to give the superintendents multiple perspectives from their peers on a dilemma. Second, it was to give them the opportunity to see how the conflicts they described might be occurring within the very room in which they were analyzing the case. Such is the theory as applied to the teaching of adaptive leadership. When writing small-group reflection papers, students in adaptive leadership classes are regularly asked if any of the dynamics present in the case were also present "in the room" in which the small-group discussion took place. More often than not, students have perceived that they are.

Hadar and Ofer (2001) have described parallel process as vividly evident in a training program in Israel, wherein the trauma of a split country, recovering from betrayals by a colonialist ally, Great Britain, was played out. The perfidy of Great Britain in turning back refugees during WWII, coupled with the strife Israel had with itself as it struggled to become a new nation 50 years following its founding, pervaded a group analysis training program (one in which the authors were participant observers, much as I was during PLS) that took place in Israel in the mid-1990s. A British "mandate" to establish a group analysis training program in Israel contained within it reverberations with post-WWI British Mandate for the Middle East, with colonialist implications. The friction that ensued in the program was, according to Hadar and Ofer, a sort of parallel process that pervaded a failed training program (p. 382). This failure echoed the failure of British promises to regions of the Middle East following the collapse of the Ottoman Empire. While such examples may appear to be far-fetched in grandeur of scale, the notion of parallel process posits that even the most sweeping historical events may echo down the years in the minutiae of smaller episodic chambers.

The notion of parallel process has been touched on in the literature on group relations over the last 70 years; it is often noted in group relations conferences and teaching in the "here and now" (also sometimes known as "case-in-point" teaching). When a superintendent was told that he was overwhelming the classroom with his interventions, he was also being given a hint as to how he was managing his district.

A similar, and somewhat related, idea is that of the "initial event." This term has often been used in psychotherapy, but it may certainly be used in other contexts as well. What Heifetz and others have called the "initial event"—often described as the psychotherapeutic session's initiating moment—is not limited to the boundary of a single unit of an individual's or a small group's actions; it may be extrapolated to the dramas of institutional disruptions on the world stage. Thus, a superintendent who began the program days later than the rest of the group in 2002 also happened to join a focus group conference call several minutes into the call several years later. In the language of adaptive leadership, the reverberations of such occurrences are broadly referred to as "data." Instructors of adaptive leadership will often say, sometimes with irony, "it's all data"—meaning that whatever is manifesting in the classroom is data from which the group can learn—not only about what dynamics are in the classroom but also about the challenges they are facing in a given district. Further discussion of "the initial event" may be found next.

Methodology

Two Methodologies

This section offers a description of the two sorts of methodologies relevant to this monograph. The first is that of the methodological approach taken to the actual teaching and implementation of PLS. In this case, the organizational behavior notion of aspirations versus realities is an apt articulation of the intended and the actual methodologies. (The reasons for the gap between what the teaching faculty and administration of this program intended as opposed to the actual outcomes is explored further later on in this chapter.)

Methodology of the Program

As an experiential leadership training program, PLS fell somewhere between a graduate seminar of intense case-in-point learning, where participants were "called out" on their blind spots and egotistical self-presentation, and the more muted atmosphere of a tightly bounded post-graduate executive training, where what are commonly referred to among teaching faculty as "conceptual vitamins" are administered to participants on a regular basis and a somewhat more immediate gratification is sought by the organizers and faculty of such programs. As such, PLS was exploring new territory. As a singular program of uncertain length of time (originally planned for approximately 18 months it extended to 2 years), the intention was to measure learning through the recording and analysis of the cases brought to the classroom for discussion in both the small- and large-group settings. Other methodologies were proposed to measure learning, yet they were not taken up. One such method, proposed by a consulting faculty member at the university, was that of asking the superintendents to keep a journal of how they used their time. Another suggestion was to interview superintendents prior to, during, and after their engagement with PLS. The research methods were minimal, however, considering the resources at hand both in terms of finances and material worthy of being analyzed and studied. In the end, two reports were written for the underwriting foundation and two written and one video case were completed.

Sense-Making

The through-line that informs the methodology of the program itself and the study of the program in its aftermath is that of narrative sense-making. This organizational notion articulates the very act of articulation and is created from an interdisciplinary area of inquiry comprised of anthropology, psychology, and organizational psychology (not unlike the notion of adaptive leadership itself). Scholars of law and society such as Ewick and Silbey (2003) have articulated the need for a narrative to be embedded in the social sciences; other scholars of narrative such as Donald Polkinghorne (1988) have asserted the necessity of narrative in society. Humanity has even been labeled a species of storytellers, *homo narrans* (Takala & Auvinen, 2016). In a similar vein, when the superintendents were asked to tell and interpret their own stories through the lens of adaptive leadership concepts during PLS, years later, when I interviewed them, they were asked to tell the story of how they remembered the program. And, in my own personal contribution, this book has emerged as a narrative object for consideration. It is meant to both hold the loosely tied ends of the project that was called PLS together in a kind of sense-making narrative and, simultaneously, to disrupt the idea of what it means to be a leader. The "collapse of sense-making" in chaotic circumstances, so well-articulated in Weick's famous case about a group of firefighters (Weick, 1993), is something that seems to occur in the professional lives of urban superintendents on a regular basis. In providing the superintendent with a new vocabulary to make sense of their worlds, PLS assisted in its reconstruction—in making sense.

Methodology of the Study

To ask a small group of participants in an executive education program tailored to their particular needs to recall, six years following the termination of that program, the effects that it had, is a natural fit for qualitative research as a general methodology. "Qualitative inquiries study how people and groups construct meaning," writes Patton (2015, p. 5). This is what the purpose of my study was—to explore how a *sui generis* group of urban school superintendents made meaning of their experience of a custom-tailored executive program. "In so doing," Patton continues,

Qualitative methodology devotes considerable attention to how qualitative analysts determine what is meaningful. Qualitative analysis involves interpreting interviews, observations, and documents—the data of qualitative inquiry—to find substantively meaningful patterns and themes.

(p. 5)

By contrast, the sort of retrospective recall and tininess of sample size is a poor fit with quantitative research; while the data here is valuable, it is not strictly generalizable. In essence, I was exploring whether or not the program had had a positive effect on a unique group of highly placed, high-profile educators. The fact that my interviews took place a number of years following the program's termination may, in fact, have enhanced the validity of its staying power. While I was looking into enormously complex systems through the lens of each individual superintendent's take on it, my research questions were comparatively simple. In the words of Professor Victoria Marsick, I was asking what they remembered of the program, and if it had had an effect on their professional practice.

The Research Questions

The research questions that guided this study were as follows:

1. What concepts of adaptive leadership did participants learn, and how did they learn them?
2. In what ways were superintendents able to apply adaptive leadership concepts learned in PLS in the context of their jobs?
3. In what ways (if any) was learning of adaptive leadership concepts similar to (or did it engender) transformative learning?

"The Study of Social Reality"

To quote Strauss and Corbin (1998): "Methodology [is] a way of thinking about and studying social reality" (p. 4). Thus, I created a descriptive case study in order to consider and study the social reality of urban school superintendents participating in the PLS leadership training program. This descriptive case study concerns itself, then, with this innovative program, and because there were multiple participants in the program, the study comprises a collection of descriptive case studies. The data collected from these case studies was culled for themes serving as the foundation for a comparative case study, data which is explored more fully in the next chapters.

The study on which this book is based was a qualitative research study, based largely on in-depth, semi-structured interviews with 8 of the original 12 participants in the PLS. I also interviewed a number of the participating superintendents' peers, as well as one of the faculty consultants (Dee's). As mentioned earlier, because of human subjects' protection considerations, I have narrowed down the number of participating school superintendents, for the purposes of this narrative, to five. This particular cohort of urban school superintendents fit the criteria for qualitative research samples according to Miles and Huberman (1994), who describe the "critical case" sample as one that "permits logical generalization and maximum application of information to other cases" (p. 28). While this group in no way approaches a generalizable sample size, I believe that their experiences, taken together, are representative of the general dilemmas of urban school superintendents (cf. Merrow, 2000).

The "case" of PLS naturally subdivided into the "caselets" of each superintendent's presumed journey of learning toward or away from operating with the aid of the diagnostic tools offered by the adaptive leadership framework, and themes emerged that mapped to certain of the terms used to describe adaptive leadership theory. As Miles and Huberman write about the tendency of cases to generate cases, even when studying one individual's experience, "a qualitative 'case,' may range widely in definition from individuals to roles, groups, organizations, programs, and cultures" (p. 29). In this way, the bounded case of a two-year executive leadership program for a small cohort of a dozen superintendents brought with it each participant's learning. To quote Merriam (1998):

> Case studies can be defined in terms of the process of conducting the inquiry (that is, as case study research), the bounded system or unit of analysis selected for study (that is, the case) or the product, the end report of a case investigation. Further, all qualitative case studies are particularistic, descriptive, and heuristic.
>
> (p. 43)

The bounded system that was the PLS program was the unit of analysis, although the unit of analysis might also be defined as each individual PLS participant's heuristic learning journey.

Interviews

As this was an exploratory case study, the interviews I conducted were semi-structured and informal. Within the context of this case, the purpose of discovering interview subjects' motives was to determine, insofar as possible (qualitatively), the degree to which their behaviors were perceived to be influenced by the PLS program. My intention was to conduct semi-structured interviews that would have a guiding purpose but that would fit Merriam's (1998) definition of the term:

> The semi-structured interview is . . . guided by a list of questions or issues to be explored, and neither the exact wording nor the order of the questions is determined ahead of time. This format allows . . . the researcher to respond to the emerging worldview of the respondent, and to new ideas on the topic.
>
> (p. 74)

The "new ideas" on the topic arose during my analysis of these interviews. As theories emerged from consideration of the data, new ideas on the topic of leadership and education began to take root. One of the key ideas of adaptive leadership as taught in the classroom—for example, the initial event—took on a life of its own when I looked back on the arc of learning that occurred during PLS.

The Initial Event

The "initial event" of the program was an unsettling one for the superintendents, as well as for me. It had to do with a directive that was given by one of the program directors to create "briefing papers" on each of the participating superintendents. For a number of reasons, I have not included any part of these in either the original study or here. Primarily, the reason for this omission is that these briefs were conducted in a way that bypassed the protection of human subjects. Although they were not part of an official or published study, had the original principal investigator been given more time to reflect on what he was asking, I suspect he would have submitted a protocol for approval. These briefs were created by a number of freelance researchers (at the time, reporting to me), and I instructed them to go out into the superintendents' districts and interview people about each of the superintendents, as well as read up about them in public documents, such as newspaper articles and school board minutes.

While these reports were reasonably well done (and some were exceptionally thorough), they became a bone of contention among the superintendents. They felt they were being kept in the dark about information that was circulating about them. Thus, the teaching team of PLS was caught, in Dean Williams' words, "on the horns of a dilemma"—whether to keep or to violate promises of confidentiality we had given to the persons we had interviewed in the superintendents' districts (D. Williams, personal communication, February 1, 2001). Because we had promised confidentiality to these individuals, we were loath to show the reports to the superintendents. And throughout the two years of PLS, the issue of the briefing reports arose, and the superintendents were somewhat mistrustful of the fact that we had conducted this kind of informal, non-sanctioned research on them. Their discomfort with what I now view as a mistake in the execution and preparation of the program speaks to the constant care with which the participating superintendents tended to their public selves. It is a tribute to the program that the overwhelmingly positive response they had to the program seemed to trump the misgivings this episode engendered. At the same time, the sloppiness of the informal reporting assignments was indicative of a carelessness that imbued the program overall.

Artifacts

Numerous artifacts endure from PLS, reports written for the foundation, briefing reports created prior to the program (described earlier), questionnaires following the program, and cassette tapes recording each session. Yet none of these, in my opinion, captures the pathos of these superintendents' dilemmas so well as a few pieces of literature. It is because these pieces of writing offer an unexpected glimpse into the lives of these superintendents that I offer them here as most representative of the program's texture.

"Shooting an Elephant"

During the last session of the pilot phase of PLS, one of the teaching faculty decided to assign an essay by George Orwell about a period in his early life when he served as a law enforcement officer in the British colony of Burma (now Myanmar). The essay, written in the 1930s, contains a telling narrative about the pressures of authority. It contains within it reverberations of the attention superintendents give to their public images.

Although well aware that he was hated, as an authority figure of the British Empire, "by large numbers of people—the only time in my life that I have been important enough for this to happen to me" (Orwell, 2006, p. 2397), Orwell describes being boxed into a corner by the population's expectations of him—hated or not. While the elephant in the story is indeed threatening to the population, the necessity of shooting it is presented as questionable. The decision to do so, however, was thrust upon him by the forces of the crowd's expectations. The "mask" he wore as a colonialist could never be removed, according to Orwell, in that situation, unless he were to become an object of mockery. The fierceness with which he sought to eschew such objectification became the fierceness that informed his action of shooting the elephant to death. The essay was an apt choice for the superintendents whose very livelihoods depended upon their public personae remaining intact. Indeed, the most outwardly and enduringly successful superintendent of the group was largely successful, in my judgment, because of his ability to maintain the composure of authority. It remains unclear the degree to which any of the superintendents in the cohort felt that their authority forced them into certain actions. What is clear is that they felt what Heifetz has called the "constraints" of authority.

The Mask Drops: Two Poems for Music Night, and "Listening to the Song Beneath the Words"

Yet in the protective environment of PLS the superintendents felt that they could surrender their need to maintain authority and explore their core, authentic selves in an exercise designed to locate core feelings about meaningful pieces of writing. By the third executive session, six months after PLS was launched, the facilitators felt that the group was ready for an experiential exercise in which participants were asked to bring a piece of writing that was meaningful to them to read aloud in a late-night session. The purpose of this exercise was to teach participants to make themselves highly vulnerable in order to connect with their audience "from the neck down." As Heifetz has often written and said, attention is the *sine qua non* of leadership (Heifetz, 1994). Getting and holding attention is difficult to do in the best of circumstances (especially in the age of instant gratification and social media); in the worst of times, it is nearly impossible. The notion of connecting emotively with others is at the crux of what Heifetz calls "the Music Exercise" (see Parks, 2005, for a fuller description).

When the superintendents convened for this exercise on Veterans Day weekend in November of 2002, they were instructed to bring with them poems and pieces of prose they intended to share with the group. After sharing them in straightforward, read-aloud fashion, they were encouraged to distill the meaning of the fragment of writing they had brought as inspirational works of art to share into a new form: the essential quality it held for them. Coached by a facilitator, they read the pieces they had brought in to share over and over, with increased feeling every time. They were then asked to sing a note or two of a made-up melody to someone else in the audience. Afterward, they considered whether or not they had been able to "hold the room" with their song.

One example of a poem that one of the superintendents brought to share with the group was Kent M. Keith's poem "The Paradoxical Commandments," a few lines of which are quoted here: "People are illogical, unreasonable, and self-centered./Love them anyway. If you do good, people will accuse you of selfish, ulterior motives./Do good anyway" (Keith, 2001). Another was Robert Frost's "Stopping by Woods on a Snowy Evening," which closes thus: "The woods are lovely, dark and deep,/ But I have promises to keep,/And miles to go before I sleep,/And miles to go before I sleep" (Frost, 1923).

While none of the superintendents was prompted, as such, to comment on this exercise in my interviews with them, Maria did. Remembering how she had been asked by the lead facilitator to sing a "lullaby" to someone in the room[1] in order to express the feeling of her piece of poetry, Maria said:

> That's . . . a memorable moment in my mind. And especially because I remember raising my hand [to volunteer for the exercise] but being very confused when I got up there as to why the hell did I raise my hand. Right? And singing a lullaby, which was . . . so strange and yet feeling comfortable doing it. You know, it was . . . very eerie.

Describing others who also stepped into the space of vulnerability, she said that she "also remembered" her fellow superintendent participants "as they were singing and struggling through that process." She also said that she understood why she thought the facilitator was asking them to step into the space of acute self-exposure by participating in this exercise.

> I think it was to help us become vulnerable, you know? And to surface vulnerabilities, but to also surface an understanding of how do you connect with people. And . . . this thing of keep—you're singing *to* [someone], and how do you connect without saying the word?

The question of how to connect with someone without saying any words is perhaps the most fundamental question of the Music Exercise and becomes a proxy for the question of how to get at the root problems in a system. Just as a piece of writing may, so the hypothesis goes, be distilled down to the essence of the feeling it carries within it, and thus become distilled, so too does adaptive leadership ultimately seek to uncover the dynamics of a system that generates a multitude of problems, causes, and conditions.

PLS Sample Schedule

Much of this chapter has been devoted to the broad outlines of the program and its purpose. Figure 3.1 is a sampling of a typical weekend-long executive program as designed by the teaching team for the cohort of superintendents. This schedule is reproduced from my notes on one of the early convenings in 2002, when the NCLB legislation was still fresh in people's minds, and superintendents were wrestling with how to implement it.

Day 1	Day 2	Day 3
	9:00–10:30 a.m. Large-Group Case: How to Shift a System under No Child Left Behind?	8:30–10:00 a.m. Strategies for Coping with Adversaries
	Break 10:30–11:00 a.m.	Break 10:00–10:30
	11:00 am–12:30 p.m. Large-Group Case: Repositioning One's Role within a Restructuring (Maria)	10:30 a.m.–12:00 p.m. Wrap-Up of Sessions What Did We Learn? How to Apply? Distribution of Evaluation Questionnaires
	12:30–1:30 p.m. LUNCH with local state education official	**BOX LUNCHES DEPARTURES BACK TO DISTRICTS**
1:00–2:30 p.m. How to Hold Authority	1:30–3:00 p.m. Large-Group Case: How to Partner with Stakeholders (Dee)	
BREAK 2:30–3:00 p.m.	**BREAK** 3:00–3:30 p.m.	
3:00–4:30 p.m. Formal vs. Informal Authority	3:30–5:00 p.m. Small Groups: Addressing Adaptive Challenges in Our Districts	
BREAK 4:30–6:30 p.m.	DINNER On Your Own	
Dinner with Guest Speaker		

Figure 3.1 PLS Sample Schedule

How the Superintendents Remembered PLS

While it is unlikely that any of the superintendents remembered the PLS schedule in its particulars, the purpose of my qualitative research inquiry was to detect patterns across individual narratives. What follows is a concise summary of the themes I was able to discern in their interviews with me.

Two main themes emerged when considering what the participating superintendents remembered of the program. Diagnosing Stakeholder Values and Managing Disequilibrium emerged strongly as the most valuable content taught to them over the course of two years. Another theme

42   Description of the PLS

to emerge was that PLS was a form of "public therapy" in terms of its teaching methods. The ways in which themes from interviews with the participating superintendents clustered is explored more fully in the following chapter.

Diagnosing Stakeholder Values and Managing Disequilibrium

Tom Swain's articulation of his learning around stakeholder values is representative of the whole group's. Like nearly all of the PLS participants, he playfully recalled the visual representation ("pizza diagram") of stakeholder values, where each slice represents a stakeholder or faction and each topping represents the values, beliefs, and perceptions of those particular stakeholder:

> I particularly remember a class meeting with [one of the PLS faculty] where he was doing . . . [the so-called pizza diagram] up on the board . . . The idea was—here's the board member—but what's behind that [person]? What's out there? Who are the board member's constituents?

Diagnosing stakeholder values came up again and again in the interviews with the superintendents as an important concept that helped them not only to think about their dilemmas but also to act upon them constructively. For instance, Bobby recalled the diagrams as "pizzas within pizzas"—a metaphor for how factions exist and operate within factions.

Bobby gave voice to the importance of managing disequilibrium. When asked what came to mind when he thought about the concepts that were taught in PLS he said, "The whole thing, adaptive change and dealing with adaptive change and how you take on and move without going too far too fast, but still keeping the heat up and the pressure up, but not blowing the top off."

And in the group interview I held with superintendents, when I asked how PLS had compared with other professional development programs they had encountered, Dee said, "Well none of the others were public therapy." The ensuing laughter implied to me that while this may have been an exaggeration of how the course was taught (the teachers/facilitators in no way claimed to be offering sessions in group therapy), it was a fair characterization, and it did not bother the participants that it had been conducted as such. There was, certainly, a general acknowledgment that superintendents are forced to "play their hands close to their chest," and that the teaching methods of the program had strongly encouraged the participants to make themselves more vulnerable and revealing. Again, Dee provides a fuller picture of this tendency, and how this went against the grain of the vulnerability demanded by the teaching of PLS:

I think superintendents by nature are not real transparent because they're guarded. And you're guarded because you balance a lot of different entities and that's how you stay alive! You stay alive by not giving [away] too much.

> And I think all that's kind of an interesting dynamic in terms of how do you have people come to this . . . understanding that what they're getting into and what they're commitment is and what their experience is going to be. Because again, as folks among us [meaning, other superintendents in PLS] described, it was like public therapy. At some point, you're baring your soul. And I don't think anyone realized that when they . . . got the grant [from Foundation R.] originally that all this was going to be happening to them.

What Was Precious, What Was Expendable

Of the five superintendents interviewed for this book, Bobby was the most articulate about what could have been added or subtracted from the program. He also gave voice to the initial negative reaction the group had to the confrontational teaching methods used by one of the lead teachers of PLS. Initially, the superintendents, who had arrived with a fair amount of resistance, were disoriented by the notions of leadership presented to them as they took in, for example, the idea that while they may have had significant positions of authority, they were not necessarily exercising leadership. When Bobby recalled the first few days of the program he said, "It's almost like [the facilitator] wants you to dislike him . . . and because it appears confrontational, and at least for us in the first meeting [of PLS] it was like, OK, so we're all wrong!" (He later invited this same facilitator out to his district to consult with him and his team.) Dee gave a more nuanced version of this feeling when she recalled that this same facilitator, who has worked with everyone from kings to heads of state to army generals, told the superintendents they were the most difficult audience he had ever had.

> And it's like, What's wrong with this picture?! But I think the conclusion was that other people sought him out, and [that] in our case it was a part of the program. And people came to it with a different mindset. [PLS] was something originally that we *had* to do [i.e., an obligation as part of a grant from Foundation R.] and once we got into it, it was like, Oh my gosh, this is so fabulous.

The superintendents also had a mixed experience working with faculty consultants from PLS who were assigned to their districts as coaching presences to create connective tissue between the learning that took place "on campus" at M University and the application of the learning in the superintendents' districts. Some of the participants were exhilarated by the experience (for example, Dee, who continued to work with her consultant after the program had ended) while others barely made contact with them. Tom came down in the middle. While he did not seem to have a particularly close relationship with his faculty consultant, he deeply appreciated the learning opportunity it afforded. PLS was, he said, "really unusual in the kind of on-site outreach element [i.e., the consultants' visits to their districts]." Had this not occurred, "it would have been a loss." When asked if he found the use of consultants valuable, Tom elaborated:

> I enjoyed [my consultant's] company, and I thought he made himself—he came to a couple of our training programs where some consultants were leading the group and had a chance to observe me and us and . . . gave us feedback in what he perceived as the evolving culture of the organization and me as a leader.

Further, he said, the consulting relationship provided "continuity" to the program. "It also," he said, "gives you a chance to practice and internalize what you're learning" when a consultant made a visit to the district and observed a superintendent in action. "So I think that was an important part of the process."

Aside from the consulting element of the program, in terms of its overall content Bobby thought there should have been greater attention given to managing labor negotiations with unions, as well as some professional development work on how to manage budgets that were getting smaller and smaller. "But the business part . . . the finance part" of being a superintendent, he said, could have been addressed more, because "budget kills." In terms of learning about what might be more "technical" kinds of work (that work entailing known problems with known solutions), Bobby thought it would have been valuable. In some cases, he said,

> You've got to come up with a technical fix. If the state's going to take away thirty million bucks, you can't say, Well, we're going to sit around and talk for a year about where that thirty million's going to come from.

Both Bobby and John spoke to the value of doing small-group work during the program and how they'd wish more had been incorporated into it. With some poignancy, Bobby also spoke to the distraction of having so much turnover among the participating superintendents. Throughout the sessions of PLS, there were only two in which the exact same participants attended. The turbulence that marks the job and the system at large was felt in the very rooms in which the program took place.

Conclusion

Earlier in this chapter, I posed the question as to how the initial event of the briefing reports debacle would inform the rest of the program. Yet perhaps the initial event lay with the larger question of how to sustain a holding environment for urban school superintendents. While the greatest triumph of the program was to create a solid holding environment, the stubborn fact of superintendent turnover was also its greatest weakness and undermined the holding environment. The fungus of this disequilibrium (i.e., the disequilibrium that results from constant turnover), which appears to be endemic to high-needs school systems, seems to have spread to the program itself, which was unable to take permanent root in the turbulent atmosphere of competition for much-needed dollars in higher education.

Note

1. As part of the exercise, the lead facilitator of PLS encouraged the individuals reciting their chosen pieces of literature to characterize the deeper "song" it represented to them. Some characterized their pieces of writing as a call to arms and others as a song of peace. Maria characterized the piece of writing she brought in to share as a "lullaby."

References

Delucia-Waack, J. L., & Fauth, J. (2004). Effective supervision of group leaders. In J. L. Delucia-Waack, D. A. Gerrity, C. R. Kalodner, & M. T. Riva (Eds.), *Handbook of group counseling and psychotherapy* (pp. 136–150). Thousand Oaks, CA, London, and New Delhi: Sage Publications.

Ewick, P., & Silbey, S. S. (2003, May). Narrating social structure: Stories of resistance to legal authority. *American Journal of Sociology, 109*(1), 1328–1372.

Frost, R. (1923). *Stopping by woods on a snowy evening.* The Poetry Foundation. Retrieved from www.poetryfoundation.org

Hadar, B., & Ofer, G. (2001). The social unconscious reflected in politics, organizations and groups: A case of overseas group analysis training. *Group Analysis, 34*(3), 375–385. doi:10.1177/05333160122077938

Heifetz, R. (1994). *Leadership without easy answers.* Cambridge, MA: Harvard University Press.

Keith, K. M. (2001). *The paradoxical commandments: Finding personal meaning in a crazy world.* Makawao, Maui, HI: Inner Ocean Publication.

Merriam, S. (1998). *Qualitative research and case study applications in education.* San Francisco, CA: Jossey Bass.

Merrow, J. (Writer). (2000, September). *Toughest job in America.* PBS. The Merrow Report. Arlington, VA: Public Broadcasting Station.

Miles, M. B., & Huberman, A. M. (1994). *Qualitative data analysis* (2nd ed., pp. 10–12, 28). Newbury Park, CA: Sage Publications.

Orwell, G. (2006). Shooting an elephant. In S. Greenblatt, M. H. Abrams, A. David, B. Lewalski, L. Lipking, G. Logan, . . . J. Simpson (Eds.), *The Norton anthology of English literature: Volume F. The twentieth century and after* (8th ed., pp. 2379–2384). New York, NY: W. W. Norton & Company, Inc.

Parks, S. D. (2005). *Leadership can be taught: A bold approach for a complex world*. Boston, MA: Harvard Business School Press.

Patton, M. Q. (2015). *Qualitative research & evaluation methods: Integrating theory and practice: The definitive text of qualitative inquiry frameworks and options*. Thousand Oaks, CA: Sage Publications.

Polkinghorne, D. E. (1988). *Narrative knowing and the human sciences*. Albany, NY: State University of New York Press.

Strauss, A., & Corbin, J. (1998). *Basics of qualitative research: Techniques and procedures for developing grounded theory*. Thousand Oaks, CA: Sage Publications.

Takala, T., & Auvinen, T. (2016). The power of leadership storytelling: Case of Adolf Hitler. *Tamara: Journal for Critical Organization Inquiry, 14*(1), 21–34.

Winnicott, D. W. (1986). The theory of the parent-infant relationship. In P. Buckley (Ed.), *Essential papers in psychoanalysis: Essential papers on object relations* (pp. 233–253). New York, NY: New York University Press. (Reprinted from the "International Journal of Psycho-Analysis," Vol. 50, pp. 711–717).

4 How Participants Remembered PLS

The purpose of this study was to examine the learning of adaptive leadership concepts that participants experienced and applied during and after the PLS leadership training. This chapter documents the major findings of the study, which answer these research questions:

1. What concepts of adaptive leadership did participants learn, and how did they learn them?
2. In what ways were superintendents able to apply adaptive leadership concepts learned in PLS in the context of their jobs?
3. In what ways (if any) was the learning of adaptive leadership concepts similar to (or did it engender) transformative learning?

The data sources were 1) in-depth interviews with PLS participants; 2) my own field notes from PLS and those taken during the process of data collection; and 3) artifacts from PLS (schedules and reading materials).

Major Challenges

The first section of this chapter comprises a description of the superintendents' major challenges that emerged thematically. The reader may wish to refresh themselves on the biographical data of the superintendents, as well as their representative cases, which are found in Chapter 2, "Portraits." You may also wish to review the brief discussion of context found at the end of that chapter, to which the following discussion refers. The challenges the PLS superintendents faced were directly linked to the context in which they endeavored to do their jobs. This section ends with an overview of how the learning superintendents experienced during PLS affected their actions in context. As mentioned in Chapter 2, the contexts that emerged most saliently (for the purposes of this discussion) were school boards, politics, the "instructional core" of districts, external mandates, and structural/ systemic change.

School Boards

One superintendent who seemed to speak for most of the others said most directly that school boards were "a constant worry in our field." Others spoke more indirectly to what Tom referred to as a structural problem of governance—i.e., that the superintendent reports to a board even though the superintendent is largely held responsible for what happens in a district. Elmore (2000) and J. T. Murphy (1991) have referred to the difficulties arising from this governance structure.

In John's case, the problems of board supervision and the factional difficulties associated with boards were compounded when the Northeastern state where he served imposed a supra-controlling board over the one heretofore responsible for his contract. Maria spoke more indirectly about conflicts with her school board and alluded to her increased "empathy" for their values. She attributed to adaptive leadership concepts the perception she held that she had become

> more conscious . . . [about] how I worked with board members, and really looking at honoring, you know, the values that they held and . . . thinking that they were [not] necessarily opposing the values that I held.

Finally, Dee also spoke indirectly to the comparative relief she now (post-PLS) experienced in not reporting to a school board, albeit she reported to "a board" that served as a governing entity for her organization. Dee emphasized that the board she reported to was made up of her "colleagues," and also made favorable comparisons between working with this entity and working with a district school board to which she reported.

A finding to emerge from the focus group interview was that of the value, or lack thereof, of the school board as a governance structure. This opinion emerged from the group gradually during our discussion. While at first the participants seemed to agree tacitly that working with a board was, in Dee's words, "an imperfect science," Maria testified to the marked improvement of a complex urban area functioning without a board—one in which the chancellor of education, overseeing a cluster of superintendents, reported directly to the mayor. The general feeling of the superintendents was that the boards failed to add value; this supports Elmore's (2000) contention that school boards are largely a reflection of the politics of their community and are thus unstable by nature:

> Since politics is not about the instructional core . . . all policy decisions are essentially about the symbolism of mobilizing and consolidating political constituencies. A smart board member, in this world, is one who spends most of his or her time using issues to consolidate political support.
>
> (Elmore, 2000, p. 8)

Politics

While superintendents for the most part spoke of the second category, politics, in terms of the group dynamics of the community, Maria spoke to the political climate during the restructuring effort in her city during the time of PLS as "difficult . . . there was change in the air. There were a lot of unknowns and people were anxious, etc. So I think that would be . . . a way of characterizing that period." This depiction seemed to describe a micro-political climate as a result of the macro-political effort undertaken in a massive organizational restructuring in a complex metropolis. Bobby also described the micro concerns of parents wanting to get their children into schools of "choice" as related to the larger budgetary climate that engendered a reduction in choices. These choices for parents had been reduced in part due to school consolidations.

> I don't know if backlash is the right word, but something close to it in terms of folks wanting to be able to get their kids into what they perceive as the better public schools and the kinds of avenues they'll take to get around the rules and regulations.

John's characterization of local politics in his district was distinctly more negative, where a zero-sum game appeared to be the prevailing motif. "I was sometimes quoted," John said, "as saying that the concept of power in [District S.] was to keep the other person from getting what they wanted, or the other group from getting what they wanted." And in Tom's case, the politics seemed to manifest both literally and figuratively. Referring to literal, "big 'P'" electoral politics, Tom described his board president as "using the board presidency as a way to platform himself" to run for public office. Tom was also acutely aware of the community's "small 'p'" politics of race when he described his hesitation to fire his black deputy.

Instructional Core

Though neither Maria nor Dee mentioned the term "instructional core" as such, both of them alluded to it as one of their main contextual concerns. Maria saw her current role as one of supporting changes to how the instructional core in her municipality was strengthened and at the same time supported.

> When a system is seeking accountability [she said, paraphrasing Elmore] . . . for every accountability that you ask of a school you need to, in turn . . . give them a resource. So it's sort of reciprocal . . . that reciprocal accountability within an organization.

Dee was more allusive, saying that an unresolved issue for her when she left her district had to do with the abiding Achievement Gap (i.e., the gap in testing scores that shows up between different student groupings) between students of color and white students in her district. The link between society's oppression of students in a minority population and the continuing lower scores of this same population was, in her view, a challenge to be met through classroom instruction. As with many districts throughout the US, underserved students in Dee's district continued to score more poorly on standardized tests than did their more privileged (often white) counterparts.

External Mandates: NCLB

While the external mandate of NCLB has affected the US education system since 2002, little mention of it was made in the interviews with superintendents. In fact, Maria was the sole superintendent to speak to the issue of working in a district in direct relation to a mandate (that of restructuring) at the time of PLS. Dee was the only other superintendent to mention external mandates, not in the context of her superintendency, but rather, in her current job as an education lobbyist. In contrast to Maria, who was working at the macro level of restructuring an entire district with hundreds of thousands of students, Dee was engaged at a more micro level of the education system in fostering mandates for teacher evaluations. Framing her work to promote a shift in mindset about the evaluation of teachers, Dee spoke of it as adaptive work: "In terms of real adaptive work," she said, "I think the [issue] I'm dealing with right now will have to do [with] effecting change and being able to change some mindsets around some policy issues."

Structural/Systemic Change

Maria and Tom were the two superintendents whose contexts seemed to embody structural, systemic change, although their experiences of this phenomenon were placed at different points on the spectrum of current education reform. For Maria, the structural change occurred within her immediate environment of a vast restructuring effort that had been under way for close to a decade (at the time of her interview), in the city where she continued to work following her retirement from her last superintendency. These changes had incorporated macro-level governance restructuring, as well as the more granular restructuring of how teachers were evaluated. Tom, by contrast, spoke of the "environment" of American education. "I don't think we are improving the quality of education in the US currently," he said, referring to the teaching of education policy in which he was currently engaged. When probed, Tom said he referred to initiatives such as compensating teachers for their students' performance on standardized tests.

Positive and Negative Influences of Contexts in Application of Learning

Table 4.1 describes the context in which superintendents operated and focuses on whether and how the application of adaptive leadership concepts seemed to positively or negatively affect how the superintendents operated in different domains of context.

This table and the discussion following it describe in what ways the learning of adaptive leadership concepts affected how superintendents operated in three broad domains of context. Two of the three are concrete: coping with school boards and engaging with the community (both imply interacting politically). The third, more abstract domain shows the greatest impact: how superintendents "got to the balcony" and began to newly perceive the overall gestalt of their superintendencies. Here the notion of "configuration" as a definition of *gestalt* is found in the *Oxford English Dictionary's* definition: "A 'shape,' 'configuration,' or 'structure' which as an object of perception forms a specific whole or unity incapable of expression simply in terms of its parts (e.g. a melody in distinction from the notes that make it up)."

Table 4.1 suggests that adaptive leadership had the most broad-reaching effect on how superintendents operate within their contexts by offering the possibility of a new or different gestalt on their challenges and situations. All of the five superintendents here discussed spoke to this phenomenon; Maria and John, in fact, remarked that adaptive leadership had given them an opportunity to view their situations as a "case" to study with the diagnostic tools offered through the teaching. Maria emphasized repeatedly in her interview that the timing of PLS was "perfect" because of the radical restructuring changes her district was enduring. It was as if the concepts offered through PLS gave her a window through which to view her situation anew: "Because I got my uh-huh, oh yeah, this is what's happening."

Table 4.1 Participant Responses: How Adaptive Leadership Concepts Affected Aspects of Superintendent Context

Suptdt.	Perception of a new gestalt	No perception of a new gestalt	School Board positive	School Board negative	Community positive	Community negative
Maria	X		X			
Bobby	X					
Tom	X					
Dee	X		X			
John	X					X

For John, the constant disequilibrium that existed in his district at the time he participated in PLS seemed to play out as a kind of petri dish in which to study how the adaptive leadership concepts he was learning played out. John described the context in which he operated in District S.:

> I guess it's fair to say it was easy to see all of the different elements of the concepts playing out because they were very real; they were very, very real—[e.g.,] the dynamic tensions, the differences, the different constituent groups, and so on and so forth. So as a laboratory, it was easy to see all of that, but it was very difficult to apply the solutions. Particularly after the [financial] control board [imposed by the governor] came in.

However, while the concepts may have come alive for John because the context worked in tandem with his participation in PLS, "it was very difficult to apply the solutions," by which he meant he found it difficult to be actually testing the concepts in a creative way in his district at the time (i.e., District S.). In fact, John seemed better able to creatively analyze the concepts and use them on the job in County K., where he was serving as superintendent at the time of his interview in 2010.

The shift in gestalt that occurred in a positive way for Bobby had to do with his adoption of the concept of discerning a "confidante" from an "ally." Whereas a "confidante," according to the precepts of adaptive leadership (Heifetz & Linsky, 2002) is someone in whom one can confide with infinite trust, an "ally" is someone with whom an acknowledgment exists (at least to oneself) that the relationship is utilitarian. As Heifetz and Linsky (2002) have written,

> Allies are people who share many of your values, or at least your strategy, and operate across some organizational or factional boundary. Because they cross a boundary, they cannot always be loyal to you; they have other ties to honor.
>
> (p. 199)

A common mistake is confusing the two roles of confidante and ally. Here again, Heifetz and Linsky articulate these relationships:

> Sometimes, however, we make the mistake of treating an ally like a confidant. Confidantes have few, if any, conflicting loyalties. They usually operate outside your organization's boundary, although occasionally someone very close in, whose interests are perfectly aligned with yours, can also play that role.
>
> (p. 199)

The use of this new vocabulary for relationships with his staff gave him a different overall view of how he was working with them. "One of the [concepts] that really did grab hold," he said,

> was the piece about [the facilitator]'s work around talking about the confidante and allies and so forth. And I think I spent more time developing allies and at least thinking about, "So who are the confidantes that I would have and that I can talk to about [certain] things . . . and feel that there's a certain level of confidentiality?" . . . and so forth.

For Tom, the overall positive gestalt on working as a superintendent informed his current job as a professor of practice, as opposed to his former job as a superintendent. The shift he seemed to want to encourage and embody had to do with shifting answers back on the questioners. Speaking of his current students he said,

> They want the professor to provide the answers and the solutions. They see me as having so much experience and having been successful, so at this point, I must know how to do this. All I have to do is give them the recipe, and all will be well. Needless to say, I don't do that.

He also spoke pointedly of using books authored by adaptive leadership pioneer Ronald Heifetz for his current teaching, and specifically mentioned *Leadership on the Line* (Heifetz & Linsky, 2002), a book which also addresses leadership as "dangerous," and explores notions of survival in leadership roles. Pushing responsibility onto one's constituents, as Tom suggested he was doing in the classroom as well as in the position he had held as a superintendent, may sometime constitute dangerous work.

Finally, for Dee, the learning overview was one of stakeholder values, wherein she attained the capacity to see that individuals are embodying a group's values. "Knowing that when we're dealing with groups it's not just the individuals with whom we're dealing . . . who people are working with, what their agenda is." Dee's gestalt shifted and emerged in a similar way to Bobby's as she began to see individuals more categorically, in the sense that she was now able to sort them into factional categories.

Two of the superintendents, Maria and Dee, expressed an ability to work more positively with their school boards as a result of learning adaptive leadership concepts. Maria spoke of having a greater understanding, like Dee, of where individuals were "coming from," and implied that before PLS she and her team were more likely to feel antagonistically toward the board when in conflict with that governing entity. Dee also spoke of using one of the PLS faculty consultants, Larry, to assist her in understanding what values various factions were resonating with within her community, and she testified to his helping her become more sensitive to issues of race in her district. Specifically, she pointed to how Larry had assisted her with her board president's concerns about equity in terms of ethnic representation in various job postings in her district.

For the category "Community" scant evidence emerged of how learning about adaptive leadership specifically affected this aspect of superintendents' contexts. John was the only one who spoke about how PLS affected his district positively in terms of community. He was the single superintendent to articulate this aspect of the program's influence on his context, and he spoke eloquently about how the program affected his ability to engage the community of District S. when he put forth an initiative to "have conversations about what needs to be the give and take [and] the development of compromises and the building of an agenda." He also seemed to have acquired a new lens on the "dynamic" nature of systems—in other words, that there were many forces acting on a system at any given time—from his learning adaptive leadership concepts.

Summary of Major Challenges for Superintendents

Certain of the many facets of superintendents' contexts emerged vividly during my interviews. My second research question asked the following: "In what ways were superintendents able to apply adaptive leadership concepts learned in PLS in the context of their jobs?" In this section of Chapter 4, the discussion has focused on how the superintendents were able to apply the learning of adaptive leadership concepts from PLS within certain areas within the contexts of their jobs. The areas of context that arose most often in discussions with superintendents were: school boards, political dynamics, the impact of the economy on budgets, the instructional core, external mandates, and structural/systemic change. The salient finding in this section was: Superintendents found that applying learning from PLS gave them an overall gestalt of their jobs, and this had the greatest impact on how they did their jobs. This new view on their jobs seemed to re-invigorate the superintendents when they discussed the experience of running their districts during and after PLS. This was perhaps most clearly articulated by Maria when she said that she could see how her district cohered into a "case" during the time she was participating in PLS.

While "getting on the balcony" was not articulated in superintendent interviews most often (see the next section, "Major Learnings"), the notion of gaining a detached view of one's situation (one that this metaphor represents), such that an overall pattern emerges to be observed, suggests that this concept took hold viscerally for several of the superintendents, although it was not reported as such.

The focus group interview reinforced the finding that acquiring the gestalt of a detached view of their situations was key to the superintendents. The bulk of this interview centered on a discussion of how these superintendents were able to see their situations more clearly due to the teachings they engaged in during PLS. An additional dimension to the finding of a shift in gestalt was the importance of the holding environment established by the cohort, and the value of discussing their cases freely with one another. Bobby spoke for the group when he said that the value of learning adaptive leadership concepts lay with

> The perspective, and the fact that we all came from a little bit different community and system, both in size and complexity and demographics, and so forth and so on—but being able to gain a perspective that really allowed us to apply some of the learning across our different contexts. And for me . . . I think that was very helpful in helping me deal with the things somebody else was doing . . . and how [another superintendent in the group] was applying some of the learning in her district. Some of that might work in my context, but . . . [I also recognized that] some of it might not.

Thus, while the areas of context that emerged were differently emphasized, throughout the group the consensus appeared to be that the ability to gain perspective emerged as a positive learning in superintendents' responses to major challenges.

Major Learnings

Diagnosing Stakeholder Values

All of the superintendents resonated with the concept of Diagnosing Stakeholder Values. This concept, along with Managing Disequilibrium, was the one most frequently mentioned—albeit, for the most part, implicitly. In essence, the job of a superintendent is to manage stakeholder values. This aspect of the superintendent's job is well documented and articulated by Elmore (2000), who has critiqued the political nature of the superintendency by using the dynamics of a superintendent's relationship to a school board as an example of the politics a superintendent must contend with "a smart superintendent is one who can count the number of board members, divide by two and, if necessary, add one" (Elmore, 2000, p. 8). While each of the superintendents spoke to stakeholder values either directly or indirectly, Maria's story was perhaps the most pronounced, reflecting a gentler approach to the politics of the job, as she spoke largely of empathizing with stakeholders who were not board members. Much of Maria's language demonstrates the pain she felt as she witnessed her colleagues' anxiety during the restructuring in her district. She also framed the case she presented during PLS, which she revisited during her interview, as that of coming to understand stakeholder values. Two quotations are representative.

The first quotation alludes to the role Maria played during the restructuring process in her district, and how she saw her role as one of "holding" the group (i.e., her peers and direct reports) around her:

> [I needed to] move everyone to go past the hurt around breaking down [the former system] and acknowledging, you know, the pain that you go through in restructuring. But also then change around "But look what's in front of us . . . and what can we craft."

While in her interview Maria was not explicit about the precise values held by these stakeholders, it is likely that the feelings of loss during the restructuring process she described had to do with the change in roles and ways of doing things that would inevitably take place in such circumstances. In a similar vein, Maria made an explicit reference to what she learned as a participant in PLS was "how to walk in the shoes of others":

> One of the things I learned a lot from [PLS] was to really put myself in the shoes of others and trying to understand their values and beliefs so that I could best try to understand [how] I could move them to where I felt we need to go as a district and . . . to change.

During her interview, Maria also made reference to the political clash that erupted between factions of her district as she created a new school. This episode echoes the central premise of what it means to engage in adaptive work—i.e., to engage in the process of trying to shift values, beliefs, and perceptions (Heifetz, Grashow, & Linsky, 2009).

Similarly, to Maria's experience, the opening anecdote of John's interview struck a chord of empathy with adversaries. As John described the circumstances under which he departed from his district in the Northeastern US, he spoke of the articulated need (for one of two boards to which he reported) to seek a new superintendent who was a person of color.

> Clearly the agenda was that they wanted a minority superintendent. I understood that; I didn't have any illusions about the fact that there was a legitimate argument to be made that the superintendent in [John's former Northeastern district] should be a person of color and that sort of thing.

When describing his own character and personality, John spoke of his aversion to conflict, and his desire to bring people together around a common purpose. At the time of his interview, several years following his move from the Northeastern district of S., John was trying to obtain buy-in from the Southeastern community (where he was then serving as superintendent) to adopt an International Baccalaureate program. This initiative was one that went against the grain of a community that relied on less-well-educated youth to seek employment in the service industry (e.g., hotels, restaurants, and bars). As John elaborated on his perception of the role of superintendent, he accentuated the presence of stakeholder values, a framework of analysis he may have received from engagement in PLS: "[For a superintendent] there are so many different constituencies with different agendas that you can't always get to where you want to get to." In a direct allusion to the teaching that went on in the program, John continued,

> That was one of the big things that [the PLS faculty were] always kind of pushing on, is that there are all of these different groups, they all have different needs, they all have different wants, and they all have different comfort levels. How can you figure out a way to engage them and get them to be all in the stew[1] and be comfortable or at least content with the sort of larger agenda that really is important for the overall community?

Tom's interview was largely concerned with issues of conflict that arose while he served as superintendent of an urban industrial center in the Northeast. He evinced little sympathy for adversaries and was mainly concerned with the governance structure of the superintendency. Like nearly all of the PLS participants, however, Tom recalled the visual representation ("pizza diagram") of stakeholder values.

Bobby's views also resonated with the concept of stakeholder values. Speaking about the complexities of NIMBY (Not in My Back Yard) issues, such as what to name a school, or which students get to attend which school, throughout his interview Bobby also alluded to the notion of stakeholder values being embedded into various factions (i.e., the notion of how a faction of different stakeholders may coalesce around a largely held value, though within that faction there might be multiple values held). More subtly, he referred to the factions within factions those diagrams represented, and how his thinking changed regarding the most effective ways in which to include representatives from different parts of the community. "I used to think that I could identify people and say, 'Well, they represent the voice of.' I don't necessarily think that anymore." Elaborating on this point, he differentiated between having a nominal representative of a certain faction of the community, such as a representative from the NAACP and working harder to find different channels of representation for different groups in the community such as the Latino community. He acknowledged that such nominal representation did not necessarily reflect the values and needs of a given community. In the following quotation, he alludes to factions within factions:

> [Nominal representatives] can represent a certain voice of a stakeholder group, but to assume that they can represent—for example, somebody ... who's from the NAACP represents the African American community.... But [we] recognize that then we need to set up a way for the larger community ... there wasn't necessarily the NAACP reflecting the entire black community. And we did the same for the Latino community. We said, "Well, let's call [an organization dedicated to the well-being of the Latin American community in Bobby's district] and ask the director ... what the Latino community thinks...." And part of that goes back to the diagram [representing the diagnosis of stakeholder values]. That actually even within the ones you have [i.e., diagrams representing factions that have the graphic appearance of a slice of pizza], that within those there is still another [faction].

Finally, Dee's interview unfolded thematically as a narrative of appreciating the articulation of stakeholder values, both in her current position as a lobbyist on behalf of urban school districts and as a superintendent coping with factions clustering around values of diversity.

As Dee described her current, post-PLS position, she referred broadly to education reform issues being brought to the attention of the state legislature of the Midwestern state where she resides and works. She described her advocacy work as "working on behalf of other superintendents." Speaking specifically about the issue of teacher evaluations based on student performance, Dee described a "dilemma" that has to do with necessitating a "change in mindset." Additionally, her work entailed "a whole agenda of education reform" that was occurring in her state, an agenda that had been brought to bear by "outside reform groups." She articulated the challenges she faced as those of trying to empathize with other stakeholders' issues as they tried to build consensus around a bill to be passed by her state's legislature.

In a more textured narrative, Dee related the story of the search for a new principal for one of the schools in her district when she had served as superintendent. In reflecting on which adaptive leadership concepts she learned, she referred directly to the concept of stakeholders representing the groups that stand behind them.

> Probably one of the things that I think is kind of an always takeaway [from PLS] that I go to often times is the learning about thinking about who people represent and who stands behind them.

The application of this concept was evident during Dee's experience of hiring a white female over a black male in a community where race showed up consistently as an issue of contention for her.

Diagnosing stakeholder values came up again and again in the interviews with the superintendents as an important concept that helped them not only to think about their dilemmas but also to act upon them constructively. The next concept to be discussed, Managing Disequilibrium, while alluded to more than spoken of directly, seemed very much a key concept for the superintendents in ascertaining various situations as they arose in their districts.

Managing Disequilibrium

The concept of Managing Disequilibrium was also articulated by all of the PLS participants, and with perhaps a greater sense of intensity than that of stakeholder values, although less explicitly. This concept relates to systemic notions of a system seeking homeostasis, similarly to the human body seeking to keep itself at a stable temperature (Girczyc, 2008, p. 41). In the context of Heifetz's adaptive leadership, the notion of how to implement what many of the superintendents (at one point or another in their interviews) referred to as "adaptive change" (as opposed to the more formal moniker of "adaptive work"), relates directly to the notion of how much disturbance a given system is able to sustain. In the PLS sessions, the idea of "turning up the temperature on a stew in order to cook it" was used as a metaphor. This cooking metaphor has also often been used for stakeholder values—for example, carrots mixing with lentils to make a stew is an image of how to work with different factions and creating a harmonious whole (R. Heifetz, personal communication, May 2001).

Maria's story, concerning the pain she felt she needed to manage in working to contain her staff's feelings, served as a paradigmatic case study of an authority figure managing disequilibrium. Maria actually used the word "equilibrium," and described how her job was to serve as a "stabilizing force" while walking the "tightrope" of knowing when to push the system toward disequilibrium, and when to try and bring it back to a state of less disturbance. More than once she described the situation in which her district was going through the process of restructuring as one of "turmoil."

> I always think about it—and honestly, the program did have a profound effect, especially around [teaching in PLS] around this whole change process [referring here to the restructuring process that was occurring in her district]. The adaptive change and the challenges that you face, and how for change to take hold—you know, how you go through this disequilibrium of the organization—to what degree do you hold it at that point and to what degree do you bring it down closer to equilibrium? And that tension that exists constantly.... And then what my role was in healing that change to sort of happen, be understood by the folks that I worked with,

and helped to be also not only the facilitator of change, but also a stabilizing force.... These were very difficult times because people's comfort level, the structures that they understood, and how they viewed the city for years and years and years—all of those were being dismantled.

Bobby spoke specifically about the clash in values over highly valued "choice" schools, and the "neighborhood schools" that were not as popular. He described his district as a university town, where espoused liberal, progressive values were not on display when it came to the residents of his district considering their own children. Summarizing an attitude he perceived as being held by the more affluent and progressive community members in his district, Bobby said, "Yes, we should have more equity.... But where it comes apart is if it's your kid." Over the 12 years of Bobby's superintendency, there were occasions when he needed to consolidate schools, or to eliminate them. This sort of action would, he said, often provoke "angst," and he also employed the metaphor of cooking a stew in describing restructuring that took place in the Northwestern district where he was superintendent.

> The decision ... to do what we call "The shaping of H. District's future" process, which actually started in '06 and went into '08 ... was also based on a lot of learning [from PLS]. ... It was the metaphor of taking the heat up, closing some schools, shutting down some choice options, and then realizing that there was still some place to go. And then subsequently deciding, Now's the time to try to go to the next level [of improvement].

In describing the incremental progress he made, Bobby spoke of the need to understand and engage stakeholder values in the process of managing distress. "And how do we do that? Engage the community to minimize the disequilibrium but have enough of it that we can actually get somewhere." In this way, Bobby described the process so often used in adaptive work—keeping the range of distress in a productive zone (Heifetz et al., 2009).

In terms of managing disequilibrium, Tom described a contentious relationship with his board, and he left a year before his contract was set to expire.

> The reason was that it was becoming increasingly apparent to me that we [the board and Tom] were going to be fighting in public all the time. The ... meetings were going to be a shouting match between me and the board president. And it just didn't seem to me that that was going to serve anybody's interest [for me to remain until my contract expired].

Tom's statement demonstrates how a superintendent might choose to manage disequilibrium by timing his resignation strategically. Tom also spoke of feeling that his district was "more or less the way I would like" at the time of his departure. So from his own perspective, the level of disturbance in the system of his district was at a manageable level.

When I asked him about critical incidents that took place earlier in his career Tom spoke of a salient racial factor: that he was the first "white guy" to assume the office of superintendent in his district in 25 years. He also spoke of some of his initial actions upon arriving in his district in terms of having to "fire or relocate three African American principals." The potential racial overtones that permeated the political realities in his district, and the consequent disequilibrium of serving as the top authority figure in education as a white male in a largely underserved African American city, became a part of Tom's calculation to manage disequilibrium that might take place if he removed a fourth African American who was highly placed in the central office as his deputy.

> Now I'm a white guy who's new in town; the first white superintendent in 25 years, and this is pretty radical. There's only one enormous high school, and I removed the high school principal. And I decided that I'd played about as many cards as I could play. . . . The deputy superintendent—who if circumstances had been different I might have put him someplace else—demoted him, shifted his role, whatever. But I didn't think I had enough credibility to pull that off. So there was a sort of political assessment there.

A "political assessment," as mapped to the major concepts of adaptive leadership, may be read as "managing disequilibrium." Given Tom's perceptions of his social and political capital, he found it impossible to fire his deputy superintendent given his race. He judged this move as too politically risky.

Dee's key anecdote involved the decision-making process regarding the hiring of a principal. As described in Chapter 2, here was at least one episode of racial tension in Dee's district. Dee's action to pre-empt the possible repercussions of making the decision to hire a white female in lieu of an African American male, she said, was made

> [J]ust because of what was happening academically with the schools; it was really important that I felt that we needed to go to with the white female. And so, rather than waiting for that to be a backlash situation, which it could have been, I could foresee people coming to the board meeting and complaining about our selection.

In Dee's judgment, the white woman was objectively more qualified than the African American candidate. In order to minimize "a backlash situation," Dee reached out to a prominent member of the African American community, "the local leader of our NAACP," in her district before this hiring decision was made widely public. This anecdote embodies a mini-case study of how to exercise leadership as an authority figure in order to manage disequilibrium.

John referred to the concept of regulating disequilibrium on three distinct occasions during his interview. The first occurred when he talked about the competing stakeholder values he contended with in his small Southeastern district (County K.) at the time of his interview. These stakeholder values necessitated managing a level of disequilibrium in the district due to the competing agendas of improving education for all students in the public schools of County K., and the desire for many of the taxpayers in that county to keep the baseline of their taxes at as low a rate as possible. John spoke of what he perceived as the importance of

> [Creating] a very high degree of pressure to move a system that is going to—innately going to—try and stay in the status quo. . . . And so there's this dynamic tension between what the students' needs are and the system's needs and the local tax-payers' [needs], who are footing the bill.

John did not consider this "dynamic tension" as something particular to his situation; he considered it "an ongoing issue that any superintendent here would have to deal with."

He also referred a second time to the need to manage disequilibrium, with regard to his own need to manage himself during a time of high stress with his team. On this occasion, John was supervising a team of grant-writers for a federal grant, and the team missed the deadline for filing the application. While this is an anecdote that might also relate to Research Question 2 (how context influenced the application of concepts), it represents an occasion where emotional disequilibrium was present and needed to be contained. John referred to his tendency to "rant and rave" when a similar situation would occur, and how his learning of adaptive leadership gave him insight into his tendencies, such that he made a decision to refrain from anger.

> I made a very deliberate decision to not get on anybody's case, to not do some ranting and raving that I might have done earlier in my career. Basically I said to the team, "Look: Didn't get [the application] in, we'll try to get them to allow us to submit anyway, we'll make the effort, but regardless of what happens with that we're going to move forward with work and all of what you basically have designed we may have to do at a slower pace, but it's what we're going to try to do anyway, and next year we can re-submit."

> So I just handled it differently. . . . And I think it was effective. I said, "Let's take the ideas, let's go back, let's start doing the things we said we were going to do anyway, whether we have the grant or we don't . . . and we may have to change the pace a little bit," and so forth.

From another perspective, we might see how John managed disequilibrium, in this case of high stakes and disappointment, as a way he exercised leadership with his team, by separating the precious from the expendable (Heifetz et al., 2009).

Finally, John also raised Michelle Rhee's failed chancellorship in Washington, DC, as an example of ineffectual leadership. While he acknowledged that the situation in Washington was in need of change, he viewed it (as did Bobby), as Rhee making too many interventions on a distressed system, overloading it to the point where she was a political liability to the mayor to whom she reported. John compared the caliber of political challenges facing the education chancellor in Washington, DC, to the difficulties he endured in the Northeastern industrial city (District S.), where he was school superintendent during the time of PLS. "Just by juxtaposition," he said, comparing District S. to the district of Washington, DC, in 2007, at the time of Rhee's appointment,

> Washington, DC, was like [District S.] for many, many years. They had too many players in the pot trying to mess with everything all the time and the superintendents that went through there couldn't get anything done until Michelle Rhee went in there and with the mayor taking control there she was able to start making a lot of really hardcore, fundamental changes in the system.

Diagnosing Rhee's mistakes, he said of her leadership: "You tried to build up too much too fast without building up a sufficient amount of consensus about where things should go." In referring to Rhee's abbreviated tenure in the Washington, DC, system (Rhee was chancellor of the system for a little over three years, resigning after the mayor who hired her was ousted in a primary election in 2010), John offered an example of managing disequilibrium by showing how *not* to manage disequilibrium. (Rhee as an object lesson in failed leadership is discussed below.)

When the superintendents spoke to the concept of Diagnosing Stakeholder Values, in general, the tone was positive. When speaking to the concept of Managing Disequilibrium, the tone seemed more negative. This made sense to me. It seems that Diagnosing Stakeholder Values is a more enlarging and empathically oriented concept, while Managing Disequilibrium is a notion of maintaining control over potential volatility, a notion that implies contraction.

Technical and Adaptive Work

The main finding about learning the theory and practice of technical vs. adaptive work was that these terms had seeped into the language of all of the participants, and thus into their thinking. Each participant used the terms "technical work" or "adaptive change." Collectively and individually, the superintendents alluded to the construct implicitly in each of their interviews.

During the focus group interview, for example, Dee referred to her current work with a state legislature as "technical work" when she expressed frustration over the legislative process in her state. Tom referred to the challenge of not firing his problematic deputy by analyzing his own actions as technical: "I did a couple of reorganizations where his role was diminished or focused. But that was technical work. That was the easy way out." And Bobby spoke at greatest length of his personal transformation, or how he viewed himself, by connecting the new language of "technical" versus "adaptive" work to how he went about his decision-making process. When asked about how learning concepts of adaptive leadership from PLS and how he applied them to his work, he said,

> I would say probably . . . it's not a specific example, because there are numbers of them that I can think of, is how I think [the program] shaped my decision in—how I look [at] decisions and not feeling like I had to make a decision right now; that I may be able to get longer term gain if I go about it and look at it as adaptive rather than a technical kind of decision.

The felt sense was that this construct, naming certain sorts of work "technical" and other sorts of work "adaptive," was a much-needed way for superintendents to articulate the dilemmas of their jobs.

Distribution of Loss at a Rate the Group Can Tolerate

The finding for "Distribution of Loss at a Rate the Group Can Tolerate" showed that four of the five PLS participants interviewed (Maria, Bobby, Dee, and John) alluded to this concept either directly (using that phrase) or indirectly. The purpose of citing this remembrance is to demonstrate, however anecdotally, that certain of Heifetz's key adaptive leadership terms had staying power many years after they were learned in the abstract setting of a classroom. Heifetz (1994) refers to this particular concept as one of exercising leadership by calibrating the extent to which a group is able to endure what it perceives as a loss of something it values. These superintendents spoke of this concept in terms of how they dealt with their constituents, and in terms of changes, they sought to make in their districts or in their post-superintendency jobs. In some cases, "managing disequilibrium" and "distribution of loss" are closely related terms, and the same anecdotes related by PLS superintendents, in some cases, were used when illustrating these terms.

When Maria spoke of her post-PLS position as executive director of a curriculum change program in a large, complex district in the Northeast, she spoke of building "connections" with the schools throughout her municipality, and how she wanted the stakeholders in those schools to "see [the changes she was in charge of implementing] as mutually supportive of them and school improvement work." Although she did not mention "distribution of loss" as such during her interview, Maria was, by implication, referring to this concept, particularly when she spoke of her work during her superintendency at the time of the program. During this time, she repeatedly spoke of her need to "hold" people through the process of change that was occurring during the restructuring process in the city.

> These were difficult times because people's comfort level, the structures that they understood, and how they viewed the city for years and years and years—all of those were being dismantled. And how to get people whose jobs were sometimes on the line, or who wondered whether their jobs were on the line to keep them focused on the student achievement piece—and making schools, you know, really support the schools—were now finding themselves in turmoil. . . . You needed to sort of help [people] understand the reasons why. Why the goal was to support the schools in a better . . . how we did need to restructure ourselves.

Maria's interview contains many references to such terms as "pain," "tension," and "turmoil"—all of which may be associated with notions of loss. That she remained in her position and was—by many reports—an effective and highly regarded superintendent (field notes, July 2001) demonstrates her understanding of exercising leadership in terms of distributing loss at a rate that people could tolerate.

Bobby's interview, which repeatedly returned to the subject of the financial challenges his district confronted, also comprised numerous references to the process of closing schools in his district. A theme emerged in his interview around the tension between closing schools and the reduction of the number of "choice" schools (selective and not open to all students equally by definition). He made reference to a "progressive" community that embodied tensions between what Argyris (1991) calls the "espoused theory" of equality for all children and the "theory-in-use," of wanting to maintain choice schools, which in many cases denied admission to the underserved student population of the Northwestern city where Bobby's district was located. In terms of "distribution of loss at a rate the group can tolerate," Bobby spoke of the need to calibrate his decisions to close schools. He made decisions to close some of the choice schools as well as some of the regular public schools in his district. He also spoke of putting together a committee that included

> All the stakeholders in terms of making recommendations and working on those recommendations [to close schools]. So I would say probably in terms of the decisions that I made trying to understand or at least judge how far we could take a certain decision at the particular time in the context we were in. And more or less, I'd say, living for another day.

His use of the term "living for another day" implies that Bobby was managing the group's (in this case, one that was made up of various disparate constituents) level of distress.

John's interview contained several indirect references to distribution of loss. Throughout the interview, he alluded to situations where distribution of loss was a part of his political calculation and decision-making process. In John's situation (serving as superintendent in a tourist destination in the Southeast), the notion of his region as a place where jobs were held primarily in the service industry, as opposed to moving toward "high end" green technology jobs, was, from his perspective, a difficult one for his community to relinquish. In introducing the more demanding curriculum of the International Baccalaureate program to his district, John implied that letting go of the service job paradigm would be difficult for various constituents in the district. It would be difficult for the taxpayers who used the district as a location for vacation homes, and therefore had little interest in raising their taxes for schools their children did not attend; it was also difficult for the year-round community residents, who believed the students graduating from the high schools had no need for a better high school education because less-well-educated high school graduates would provide labor for the service industry.

> The political or practical environment [in County K.] is that there are people who will argue that, well, we have to have a sufficient number of students who graduate from the high school who are going to work in the hotels, in the vacation industry, and do those kinds of jobs, and therefore why do we need to do this math and science and I.B. [International Baccalaureate program] and all that kind of stuff? We need our workers.

A second instance of distribution of loss concerned the political climate of John's district, District S., where he served as superintendent during PLS. From his perspective, the way in which competing factions operated concerned distribution of loss implicitly, where one faction's loss was another's gain. In such a climate, John found it difficult to ask for people to endure change that would entail any kind of loss.

The next two concepts to be discussed, "Getting to the Balcony" and "Staying Alive," are given briefer treatment here as fewer participants discussed these in their interviews. When they did so, they gave the concepts less consideration than the previous four.

Getting to the Balcony and Seeing the Dance Floor

The notion of "getting to the balcony and looking down on the dance floor" was alluded to by John. The terms "in the stands" and "on the court" have been used to convey the same meaning by Erhard, Jensen, Zaffron, and Granger (2012) as metaphors for getting perspective on what is happening "from above" while in the midst of engaging in action in a given system. The image of the "balcony view" is used by Heifetz (1994) in describing how to distance oneself from a situation and to see patterns of interactions among individuals and groups. As discussed in the previous section of this chapter, this image served as an analogy in the discussion of how the learning of adaptive leadership offered superintendents a useful gestalt on their jobs and situations. John referred to it implicitly when describing his experience of the Northeastern district.

John's comments about "getting to the balcony" were inferred by me. Much of his description of the learning he gleaned from PLS concerned seeing his district anew in light of the program. I would consider such learning as a way in which John was "getting in the stands," in what was often referred to by him as a confusing situation in his district.

As Getting to the Balcony (and the concept that follows, "Staying Alive") was not as richly discussed as the first four concepts in this section, I would speculate that the particularistic language used for these terms may have been less memorable than, say, "pizza diagrams" and "technical versus adaptive" work—terms that might fit more easily in the vernacular.

Staying Alive

Two of the PLS participants—John and Tom—spoke directly about, or alluded to, the notion of "staying alive" in their jobs, although John was not explicit in his discussion of this concept. Tom, by contrast, alluded to "staying alive" in his superintendency mostly in reference to his decision to resign his superintendency before his contract expired in order to accept an offer to teach. "I knew that the [chair of the board] had the votes on the board to put a thumb on me if he wanted to."

I have noted that Tom used Heifetz and Linsky's *Leadership on the Line* (2002) for his teaching syllabus. As has also been noted, the main topic of this book is the notion of how leadership is dangerous and offers strategies throughout the text to "stay alive" while leading. The story

Tom told of his departure from his district demonstrated that he wished to leave his superintendency of his own volition and thus strengthen his viability as a potential employee elsewhere—therefore, "staying alive" professionally.

Other adaptive leadership concepts that certain of the PLS participants alluded to as key learning were as follows:

- Orchestrating conflict—Tom, and John
- Listening for the music beneath the words—Maria
- Parsing the difference between formal and informal authority—Maria

These findings are not discussed at length because they were so briefly touched upon. In terms of "orchestrating conflict," John explored this concept most fully when he spoke about the need to generate tension in County K. by introducing the I.B. program. And Maria made a subtle distinction between formal authority (what she called "sitting in the seat") and informal authority (what she referred to as "influence").

Unexpected Findings

Two additional findings that emerged from the interviews demonstrated a level of absorption in learning adaptive leadership concepts. The first concerns the emergence of Michelle Rhee's tenure as Chancellor of the Washington, DC, public school system; the second concerns discussions of race and class. The theme regarding Rhee's tenure emerged as an object lesson in how *not* to exercise adaptive leadership. Issues of race and class appeared to be natural outcomes of the critical reflection the superintendents engaged in during PLS and during their interviews.

The Case of Michelle Rhee

Two of the superintendents—Bobby and John—referred to Michelle Rhee's abbreviated tenure as Chancellor of Education in Washington, DC, as an object lesson. They both referenced her demise as exemplifying that of an urban superintendent unable to manage the politics of her district as a reformer. John spoke thus about her:

> Now, ultimately, she got thrown out because there were too many constituent groups that said, "Enough. We're not going there. We're not giving up this, we're not giving up that." So it probably was a classic study in some of the concepts [in her case] because, ultimately, they voted the mayor out and she had to go. But, basically, they said, "We're not going there. You tried to build up too much too fast without building up a sufficient amount of consensus about where things should go."

In terms of what many of the superintendents termed "adaptive change," Michelle Rhee was, in both his and Bobby's view, unable to apprehend or operationalize it.

Race and Class

All of the superintendents raised issues of race, class, or equity in their discussions of the effects of PLS. These issues arose in the interviews intermittently. Several of the superintendents saw defending the rights of minority and underserved students as important causes in their districts, while others raised issues of racial tensions within their districts.

The superintendents who addressed issues of equity in their districts were Maria and Bobby. Both spoke passionately about their desire to serve the needs of underserved students; they also identified themselves as part of a minority group.

For Maria, the issue of equity arose as she recounted the story of creating a new school in the district where she served as superintendent prior to the education restructuring of her municipality. In this "case," Maria recounted the efforts she had made to work with two different factions of her district to create a new technology-themed school that would satisfy the needs of the more affluent families and simultaneously be available to the less-well-off students in the neighborhood. Her testimony suggested that she used the concepts of appreciating the values—in a positive light—of other factions or adversaries while seeking to resolve the issue of creating a new school that would satisfy vying constituents.

Of the four superintendents, Bobby (the sole African American male in the group) spoke most extensively and most passionately about issues of class equality in his district. His was the only interview in which the greatest proportion of the conversation centered on issues of equity. Bobby described his district as largely populated by "progressive" professionals who believed in equity except when it came to "*their* kids." He expressed amazement that people would speak openly about purchasing houses in certain neighborhoods so as to ensure their children's eligibility to attend certain schools. "I mean we've had folks who admit publicly that because they have the wherewithal they've gone and bought a house in the different part of town, so they could send their kids to a particular high school." As with Maria's case, a key anecdote Bobby recounted during his interview was the same one as the "case" he presented during PLS, which had to do with honoring a civil rights worker and hero by naming a school for him.

One issue of equity, the Achievement Gap—a construct that has been foregrounded by educators since the advent of NCLB—was mentioned in passing by all of the superintendents either implicitly or explicitly. I consider this education issue a part of education policy and therefore as one that falls outside the rubrics of race, class, or equity. Thus, while the remaining three superintendents all addressed issues of race, their mention of the Achievement Gap does not appear to be in any way exceptional. The additional findings that follow concern race from the perspective of individuals who identified themselves as Caucasian: Tom, Dee, and John.

The theme of race among these three superintendents emerged as an issue they had to contend with. The issue was foregrounded in Tom's interview when he spoke candidly about being the first "white guy" to serve as superintendent in his district in 25 years. Two anecdotes stood out as related to racial tension in his district: The first concerned his relationship to his African American deputy, and the second concerned a conflict with a new African American board member responsible for the investigation of corruption on Tom's part. Both anecdotes, from Tom's perspective, had racial overtones that were the fundamental sources of these conflicts.

Dee also spoke candidly about race in her descriptions of challenges encountered with her community and on her board. Her encounter with the African American board member whose overriding concern was giving more African Americans jobs in the school system is a case in point. Dee's anecdote regarding her application of adaptive leadership concepts to how she did her job concerned her controversial decision to hire a white woman over a black man for principal in her district. Her testimony suggests that Dee gained a wider awareness of how racial tensions were present in her district.

Finally, John talked about a racial issue at the beginning of his interview. He had been forced out of the district of his first superintendency and spoke of the perceived need to place a minority superintendent in his position as something he "understood," albeit he was disappointed that he could not finish the work he had started in the district. "I don't have any illusions about the fact that there was a legitimate argument to be made that the superintendent in [his district] should be a person of color and that sort of thing."

Summary of Major Learnings

I have subdivided this summary into three parts: 1) learning reported by individual superintendents, 2) learning reported by the focus group, and 3) unexpected findings.

Learnings Reported by Individual Superintendents

The findings regarding major learnings gleaned from the teaching of adaptive leadership concepts in PLS, as reported in participant interviews and applied to their understanding of their jobs, revealed more frequent mentions of learning around the concept of diagnosing stakeholder values, managing disequilibrium, parsing the difference between technical and adaptive work, and distribution of loss at a rate the group can tolerate, with less frequent mentions of learning around staying alive. The least frequently mentioned topics were orchestrating conflict, listening for the music beneath the words, and making meaning out of the difference between formal authority and informal authority. All of the concepts mentioned suggested a positive effect of the learning superintendents experienced.

Learning Reported by the Focus Group

Within the focus group interview, the main adaptive leadership concepts mentioned reflected those discussed in the individual interviews: diagnosing stakeholder values and technical vs. Adaptive work. The latter concept was merely touched upon by Dee (during her interview she made a comment in passing that the state legislature she was working with was making her impatient by being bound up in "technical work"). The tacit understanding of this term evinced by the group implied that a key learning for them was the difference between technical work and adaptive challenges.

Diagnosing Stakeholder Values arose briefly but intensely in the focus group interview and was alluded to in the context of board relations. When I asked if "any of the learning helped them deal with their boards,"[2] the response was a universal affirmative. At this point in the conversation the dialogue turned to the "pizza diagrams," (depicted as a circle with wedges in it, often used to illustrate the concept of stakeholder values, wherein each wedge represented a faction that clustered around values of various stakeholders):

TOM: I still remember, what were they, daffodils or something or another?
ME: I think [we] called them "pizza diagrams."
BOBBY: The pizza diagram.
TOM: Yeah!

The conversation then quickly circled back to the challenges associated with working with boards, and there was universal agreement that they were, at best, "a necessary evil."

Thus, the density of conversation around stakeholder values during the focus group interview (as the subject the group stayed with the longest during its discussion) reflects individual learning—all of the participants resonated strongly with this concept.

Unexpected Findings

Finally, the unexpected findings that arose branched off into two directions: the emergence of the case of Michelle Rhee and the emergence of the issues of race and class. Of interest to me was that the superintendents who raised the question of Rhee's chancellorship were both male. Albeit Rhee has been criticized strongly for her management of the DC public school system for the brief time she was there (see Starnes, 2011), the gender bias against her reflects current research on bias against women occupying positions of power (Okimoto & Brescoll, 2010; Sandberg, 2013). And while most of the superintendents discussed race and class issues (with no prompting questions from me), those who raised the issue of race as problematic to their personal positions identified as Caucasian. The remaining superintendents to raise the issue of race *and* class in the framework of equity were persons of color.

Adaptive Leadership as Seen Through the Lens of Transformative Learning

For the purposes of this section, I have focused on the most essential aspect of transformative learning, which is the discarding of old assumptions and the attainment of a new perspective on self and consequent behaviors. Mezirow (2000) and Cranton and Roy (2003) have broken down transformative learning into distortions of habits of mind (or, as I would call it, *shifts in perspective*) into six basic types: epistemic, sociolinguistic, psychological, moral-ethical, philosophical, and aesthetic.[3] The process of transformative learning may be distilled into four basic steps, gleaned from Mezirow (1991, 2000): 1) experiencing a "disorienting dilemma", 2) engaging in critical thinking, 3) reintegrating new concepts into a new way of being, and 4) integrating new perspectives with old.

In my view, all of the participants' reports of their experiences of PLS discussed here were suggestive of transformative learning. Because I was unable to create a study with clear benchmarks for participants' mindsets and orientations prior to PLS, I could not credibly draw conclusions or ascertain whether and if transformative learning took place definitively. The findings for how the learning of adaptive leadership occurred may be viewed, however, through the lens of Mezirow's model of transformative learning, in a continuum that spans the most fully described changes to the least descriptive answers. In this sequence, the findings from my interviews with participants are presented next in two subsets: those relating to the six shifts in perspective and those relating to the four basic steps.

As transformative learning was not the primary research focus for this study, and as the study was not designed specifically to measure transformative learning, there is clearly a limitation on the findings for this question. Yet this area of the findings is certainly rich.

Table 4.2 demonstrates the kinds of perspective shifts superintendents showed evidence of experiencing as they went through the process of

Table 4.2 Participant Responses: Findings on Shifts in Perspective

Superintendent	Sociolinguistic Learning	Psychological/ Behavioral	Moral/ Ethical	Epistemic	Philosophical	Aesthetic
Maria		X				
Bobby	X	X				
Tom	X					
Dee	X	X	X			
John	X	X	X			

learning and applying concepts of adaptive leadership of their PLS training. Four out of five experienced a shift in "sociolinguistic perspectives," which, in this case, describes how they used language in the interview and how they reported using language of adaptive leadership in their districts. Four out of five also indicated that they sensed having undergone some sort of psychological and/or behavioral shift as a result of PLS. Here I linked suggestions of psychological transformative learning with apparent shifts in behavior—or, in Saavedra's words, "Action, acting upon redefinitions of . . . perspectives . . . [as an] indication of transformation" (Saavedra, 1995, as cited in Mezirow et al., 2000, p. 295). Two of the five alluded to an enhancement of moral/ethical learning, or what might simply be called awareness, as a result of participating in the program. In the category of "moral/ethical" changes in perspective, two of the superintendents articulated perceptible shifts toward greater awareness of "the right thing to do" as a result of their participation in this adaptive leadership training program. None of the superintendents made reference to any sort of epistemic, philosophical, or aesthetic shifts in awareness or perspective.

The following discussion addresses the superintendents' learning experience as seen through the given facets of transformative learning. While Table 4.2 distinguishes among implied discrete perspective shifts, here the discussion pertains to one or more perspective shifts together, as these shifts often seemed to overlap.

Maria. I found scant evidence of sociolinguistic learning in my interview with Maria—i.e., that she had actually adopted the language of adaptive leadership. However, she emphasized the felt need for empathy she experienced during the transition in and transformation of her district. When I asked if any of her behaviors or habits of mind had changed as a result of participating in PLS, Maria responded that she felt she had become more empathic and more aware of how to lead "by influence" (i.e., from a position of informal authority). "So I think what I've learned also is that whole notion of leading by influence rather than sitting at the seat." By this statement, Maria perhaps meant she learned how to use informal authority over formal authority, which suggests psychological behavioral as opposed to sociolinguistic shifts.

Bobby. Bobby demonstrated learning through his understanding of his challenges and in his descriptions of how he met these challenges, in both his general recollections and in specific anecdotes he shared. Speaking about the impact of the program as a whole, as discussed earlier in this chapter, Bobby said that what remained with him most clearly were the adaptive leadership concepts. When asked what he meant by this he elaborated: "The whole thing, adaptive change and dealing with adaptive change and how you take on and move without getting too far too fast, but still keeping the heat up and the pressure up but not blowing the top off."

He also spent a substantial portion of his interview discussing the critical incident of naming an elementary school for a civil rights leader, demonstrating a more direct sociolinguistic shift in perspective. As Bobby articulated his experience of making an effort to bring in different factions, and realizing that one representative of a community group did not necessarily represent an entire community, I noted that he again invoked the "pizza diagrams," a trademark image for Heifetz's adaptive leadership theory about the importance of recognizing and understanding factions that cluster around stakeholder values.

So Bobby's interview testimony suggested he had experienced transformative learning both socio-linguistically (i.e., by using specific language associated with adaptive leadership) and psychologically, particularly in his evolution as a leader within his community, as a result of the program.

> I think I probably looked at everything as a *technical problem* and I had to have the solution. I had to be the answer guy. I eventually had to have the answer because that was what, as superintendent, I was expected to do [emphasis added].

In making a distinction between how, after PLS, he conceived himself as other than "the answer guy" with "technical solutions," Bobby implied that he was acting differently as a result of his engagement with PLS. This implication demonstrates the notion of transformative learning as "action upon redefinition of our perspectives" (Saavedra, 1995, as cited in Mezirow et al., 2000, p. 297).

Finally, in another anecdote related to the initiatives Bobby undertook in order to create more equity in terms of schools being available for *all* children in his district—specifically, by making recommendations to the school board to close certain schools—Bobby described a different reaction from one he might otherwise have had. A group of teachers proposed a merging of a "choice" and a non-choice school as an alternative to closing one of them. "I'm not sure that before the [PLS] program I would have been open to letting them [merge the schools] or going back and reversing a recommendation that I had already made to the board and [that] they had accepted." This self-disclosure suggests a general shift in mindset or perspective.

Tom. Tom's transformative learning was difficult to identify because he entered PLS with a degree of psychological theoretical self-knowledge. It was consistently challenging, during my interview with him, to locate learning or a change in his own behavior that could be traced to the program. Throughout his interview, Tom evaded direct questions about his learning in the program and gave indirect answers about its influence. With regard to his sociolinguistic learning, he said that "the shadow of Heifetz [i.e., the theory of adaptive leadership] has passed through" when he spoke of his own teaching at the time of his interview, and he claimed to use Heifetz's books for his courses. For my part, I would speculate that transformative learning may have happened, at least in the realm of sociolinguistic habits of mind, despite the shallowness of evidence from Tom's interview.

Thus, despite the dearth of data in Tom's interview on transformative learning, there was a specific episode he attributed to the learning of adaptive leadership, which was his recommendation that a subordinate principal undergo an experiential leadership training program at the Center for Creative Leadership. "I think that I was able to have the conversation with her in a way that was empathic; it wasn't particularly judgmental, I think, in a way that I hoped help her feel that she was being supported." Similarly to Maria, Tom ascribed an enhanced capacity for empathy to his experience of learning adaptive leadership concepts.

Dee. Dee indicated having undergone transformative learning in terms of a shift in perspective as described by Saavedra (1995, as cited in Mezirow et al., 2000, p. 297), which implies a change in action as the result of change of perspective. It was clear that the learning of adaptive leadership had caused a shift for Dee in terms of how she framed situations (again, I am reminded of her exclamatory "talk about technical work!" as the way she described the state legislature's *modus operandi* during the focus group interview), and equally clear that she had used language of adaptive leadership to articulate challenges, implying a sociolinguistic shift in perspective. The locus of Dee's interview was centered on a change in the way she perceived herself and went about the business of running her district. This change suggests that a psychological shift in perspective occurred for Dee.

When asked about a change in habits of mind, Dee spoke of having a twofold psychological shift in perspective. The first shift involved becoming what she termed "less naive." As one of the new superintendents in the cohort, Dee remembered being characterized as "refreshing" by one of the faculty, as she appeared to have a less "cynical" view of the superintendency. She described her enthusiasm for the adaptive leadership concepts as "Pollyanna-ish." By the time PLS came to a close, she said, "I wouldn't say that I left being more cynical, but I think by being in the program, by listening to other people's experiences, I became more realistic about a lot of things."

The second shift Dee described centered on becoming a more critically reflective thinker, which suggests a deeper transformation in her habits of mind. Dee attributed this change to the fact that she had a faculty consultant from PLS, Larry, come to her district and observe her in action and in meetings.

> Because he would come and literally watch me work and attend events with me and sit in meetings and that kind of thing. And then when we would talk about it afterwards sometimes he would just really push. About why I thought something was as it was—or if I was being defensive—he would call that out.

Finally, Dee was very positive about the impact these challenges to her thinking had on her way of approaching issues differently in her district, particularly with regard to race. She said that often Larry would point out the racial issues happening in her district and help her look more deeply at what a particular person's reaction might represent.

> [Larry] would often help me focus on [issues that] would oftentimes [be] around racial issues, where sometimes there would be certain individuals in your community that kind of always had the same thing to say or always poke the same places or whatever. And so sometimes you just didn't give them as much due as you should or just say, "Oh, that's whomever, and that's kind of what they always say." And [Larry] would oftentimes help me to stop and really look deeper into what they were trying to say—what the issue was.

And, as discussed earlier, a critical incident for Dee occurred when she took extra care to consider the political repercussions that might have occurred in her hiring the white female over the African American male for a key position in her district; this inferred, to me, that Dee's sensitivity to racial issues in her district was possibly a sign of her transformative learning, in that her actions were now informed by new ways of making meaning.

John. John was perhaps the most self-reflective of the superintendents when considering the question of whether or not learning adaptive leadership had changed his general mindset. When asked if "there was any shift during or after PLS" in his "mindset," which I define as a constellation of "values, perceptions, approaches that you would take to anything," his immediate response was, "good question." He attributed the capacity to reflect more on how he managed his "demeanor" to learning adaptive leadership concepts; in particular, he focused on anger and how he affected other people as a leader. Speaking of his career in education, he said,

> I came to some realizations . . . that my capacity to lead and persuade other people was very much depending on my attitude and what kind of demeanor I was presenting to people I was working with. So as a consequence of [these realizations] I think I've been much more conscious of that and have been kind of working on making sure that my—there are certain things that frustrate and anger me in the process of working on change and bureaucracy and people kind of sitting back and not moving things forward. So I've kind of worked on not showing anger as much as I did earlier in my career and trying to deal with things in a different kind of way.

In describing "dealing with things in a different way" John used the example (previously cited) of the episode during which his team was working on a grant application and missed the deadline (see "Managing Disequilibrium"). To use again the construct of research as a kaleidoscopic lens, this incident may be viewed as possible evidence of behavioral transformative learning, as well as one in which John managed the disequilibrium of failure to meet a goal successfully.

With regard to suggestions of moral/ethical learning, John and Dee were the superintendents most focused on this aspect of their behavior when reflecting on their learning from PLS. John's self-inquiry around his proclivity toward anger and frustration implied moral consideration. Dee's decision to hire a white female instead of an African American male was morally the "right thing to do" for her district and seemed to be tinged with a sense of moral duty to her district.

Summary: Suggestions of Possible Transformative Learning for Superintendents

The previous section has explored evidence of suggested types of transformative learning for the PLS superintendents. The following section explores adaptive leadership *as seen through the lens* of transformative learning and is concerned with *steps taken toward* it. In Table 4.3, the basic four steps of the process of transformative learning (as opposed to the kind of transformative learning that may or may not have taken place) are outlined.

Steps Taken Toward Transformative Learning

Data in this sub-section of Chapter 4 are broken down into four categories of basic steps in the process of transformative learning. This section addresses the question as to which steps superintendents appeared to have undertaken toward potential transformative learning.

78 How Participants Remembered PLS

Table 4.3 Transformative Learning: Steps Taken

Pseud.	Disorienting Dilemma	Critical Thinking	Reintegration of Concepts	Integrating New Perspectives with Old
Maria	X	X	X	X
Bobby	X		X	X
Tom				
Dee	X			
John		X		

The four steps of transformative learning outlined in Table 4.3 approximate the order in which they would occur for someone experiencing transformative learning, beginning with "disorienting dilemma." Evidence of this initial phase of transformative learning appeared for most of the superintendents during the first session of PLS, when one of the lead faculty for PLS, Richard Blair (a pseudonym), adopted a confrontational approach to teaching the cohort (Field notes, May 8, 2002). Four of the superintendents referred to this teaching style as "off-putting," and Bobby spoke for many of them when he said, "If [my opinion of the program's value] was based on the first session that we had with Blair, I would say, 'Don't ever bring that guy in again!'" The general consensus among the superintendents was that Blair had made them feel inadequate as professional people and had left them with an unsettled sense of themselves as superintendents. Dee also alluded to the way in which Blair interacted with cohort members and seemed to make them deliberately uncomfortable. Yet in the sense of disorientation for the sake of learning, Blair was acting as a "change leader" who "should 'disturb' the system," according to Burke, Lake, and Paine (2009, p. 72). The PLS participants came to recognize the value of Blair's confrontational methods—frequently used in the teaching of adaptive leadership—as, in Dee's words, "public therapy," which made the adaptive leadership case-in-point teaching methods unique.

Critical thinking is an integral part of transformative learning (Brookfield, 2000), and two superintendents, Maria and John, considered their own manner of thinking as a way to address the needs of their communities and constituencies. For Maria, this kind of reflection led to an empathic approach toward any faction she felt in conflict with, represented by her board. She spoke of needing to "really take an introspective look at what we were doing and whether we were addressing [others' needs] or not." John also observed a conflict with his board and discussed his decision not to fight their agreement on not to renew his contract (this was the supra-board imposed on his district by the state).

An element of introspection was present in his description of how he came to that decision.

> So I don't like being a polarizing leader. . . . I don't like the notion of being a lightning rod for dividing the community. . . . So I'd much rather just try and bring people together and create unity of purpose rather than division.

In this instance of self-reflection, John noted to the researcher the process of critical thinking that informed his decision not to fight for an extension of his contract (which had been backed by his local school board).

The notion of "reintegration of concepts into a new way of being" overlapped in many cases with "integrating new perspectives with old." The same superintendents—Bobby and Maria—seemed to experience these steps most distinctly. Maria spoke of having a new sense of herself (and, thus, a new way of being) as she managed conflict over the creation of a new school in her district.

> I think that throughout that process I was in [PLS]. . . . I think it helped to help me to sort of manage . . . a way that I could find equity for all and be able to address the needs of the communities.

In terms of integrating new perspectives with old, Maria spoke of valuing influence as a skill "rather than sitting at the seat"—i.e., having a certain position of authority in an organization.

Bobby commented more directly on learning concepts of adaptive leadership and using them actively in his district.

> We did a lot of work in our district around adaptive leadership and those kinds of things. We did work with our board on it. . . . Even . . . about labor relations in business and even how you do budgeting and stuff.

Bobby indicated here that while he was seemingly reintegrating the concepts of adaptive leadership into new ways of being, by doing work with his board using the concepts, evidence of a perspective change is also apparent. He also said that superintendents are "looking for a technical solution while living in an adaptive world," and that "It all comes together around how do you do adaptive leadership and lead for change."

Summary of Findings on Adaptive Leadership as Seen Through the Lens of Transformative Learning

This section on adaptive leadership, as seen through the lens of transformative learning, contains a nuanced discussion of superintendents' perceptions of themselves. Because this study is based on retrospective recall, the data were heavily reliant on memory and perceptions. Thus, any claims of transformative learning must be considered suggestive.

The findings on transformative learning also add dimension to how superintendents experienced a new gestalt on their jobs. Sociolinguistic shifts in perspectives articulated more deeply how these gestalts emerged. In terms of what may have been psychological shifts in perspective, two superintendents attested to such shifts in particular depth: John and Dee. It was evident to a lesser extent that Maria and Bobby underwent such shifts, while Tom's perspective changes, in this aspect, remained enigmatic.

Of the four steps of transformative learning addressed in this section, the "disorienting dilemma" of confrontational teaching methods employed during PLS emerged as resonating with the group most strongly. This finding was reinforced in the focus group interview (where no questions were asked about individual experiences of transformative learning), when the superintendents laughingly agreed that PLS was a unique program—again, in Dee's words, akin to undergoing "public therapy." Their sense was that the personal aspects of the program were initially disorienting, that the value of this approach had a lasting impact and had thus transformed their views of themselves and their jobs as superintendents.

PLS as Professional Development

Traditional notions of professional development, according to Drago-Severson (2012), "often seek to increase adults' fund of knowledge or skills (*informational learning*)" (p. 6, emphasis in the original). The idea of informational learning relates to Heifetz's notion of technical work (Drago-Severson, 2012, p. 8). In the literature on transfer of training (to be explored more fully in the next chapters), this kind of professional development might be called training with the aim of "low-road transfer" (Salomon & Perkins, 1989, as cited in Yorks, 2003, p. 150), which is to say, using less abstract applications of learning to context—or, in Yorks's words, "straightforward application of behaviors learned in one context to another with little modification" (p. 150). This is the sort of professional development that has been decried by Levine (2005): "There are myriad non-degree professional development programs that are supposed to update and expand administrators' knowledge of the field, raising their salaries in the process" (p. 22).

Drago-Severson (2012) advocates the sort of professional development for educators that might address the adaptive challenges with which aspiring school leaders are faced. "The current educational climate calls for new approaches to support adults and their growth so that they can meet these new leadership demands and be even more effective leaders" (p. 8). PLS was the sort of program that would fit Drago-Severson's prescription for "a new model that explicitly prepares leaders to better manage the complex challenges they face in schools" (p. 8). While PLS's curriculum stemmed from a broader orientation, including more "leadership" (versus an "educator" orientation), and while it did not grant a degree or even a certificate in training, it fits within the parameters of professional development as a "leadership training program" for an elite group of urban school superintendents. It complies also with what Aguinis and Kraiger (2009) refer to as a combination of training and development, in that it had specific programmatic aims of teaching certain concepts to enhance efficacy, while also comprising "activities leading to the acquisition of new knowledge or skills for purposes of personal growth" (p. 452), such as role-playing difficult conversations.

Among the questions posed for this study was one that asked the superintendents about a hypothetical redesign of PLS. In every interview, this question was accompanied by a question (either directly asked or implied) about how PLS compared with other professional development in which PLS participants had engaged. In this section of the chapter, we explore the findings on how the superintendents perceived of PLS as professional development. Table 4.4 offers representative quotations regarding PLS as professional development, both within the individual interviews and, when pertinent, in the focus group interviews. In cases where a superintendent did not offer any opinion on PLS as professional development, a horizontal line fills the box. (As John was unable to participate in the focus group interview, "N/A" appears next to his name in the column for quotations from the focus group interview.)

While other sections in this chapter have discussed the findings from the focus group toward the latter part of the section, the findings for this section begin with the group because the discussion of PLS, as compared with other professional development programs, was the culminating point for the superintendents able to participate in the group interview.[4] During the individual interviews, superintendents also compared PLS favorably with other professional development, although they did not go deeply into the subject. During the conference call, their collective enthusiasm emerged. Bobby seemed to capture the feeling of the group when he said that

> [PLS] was the only [professional development program] I really anticipated and looked forward to getting together ... and having not only the value of the program but the value of the collegiality, and it's one that I know that I missed when it was over.

Table 4.4 Superintendents' Perspectives on PLS as Professional Development

Superintendent	Representative Quote (Individual Interview)	Representative Quote (Focus Group Interview)
Maria	"PLS helped me become stronger at understanding my role during the [restructuring] change [in my district], and how to support the change."	Agreed that PLS was a "very unique experience." (positive)
Bobby	"I think that . . . one of the things that affected me most was that I didn't have to have all the answers."	"[PLS] was the only [professional development] I really anticipated and looked forward to getting together and having not only the value of the program but the value of the collegiality, and it's one that I know that I missed when it was over."
Tom	"This is the first time I've been in a [professional development] situation where I really felt I could let loose about some of my own [personal] concerns."	Did not think he could compare it to other professional development programs. "A unique experience." (positive)
Dee	"Many of us thought at the time that [we were participating in PLS] . . . here was something very special about [PLS] that really needed to be documented and figure out a way to replicate that."	[Speaking of lobbing Foundation R. to continue funding PLS] "because I did think . . . there is something here that was unusual, that I don't think has existed before or since . . . because I think each of us would say that things that we learned [during PLS] we've been able to take and apply to many other situations."
John	"I got a lot out of it . . . on the cognitive level, I learned a lot; the interactions with the other superintendents were great; I had really good mentoring from [my coach] on a number of things."	N/A

Although Dee joked about the program being "public therapy," her tone was positive, and throughout the focus group interview she made a point of saying how much she appreciated that the research of my study was capturing what took place during PLS; without prompting, she also spoke about how she had urged Foundation R. to re-convene PLS in its original form. Dee said,

> Because I still think there is . . . also said that, that's why, Sarah, I'm glad you're doing this piece [i.e., collecting data on the program participants' learning] because I did think—I know this wasn't necessarily their intent or [the foundation's] main focus—but there is something here that was unusual, that I don't think has existed before or since. And I think it was worth writing about, and I think [PLS] was worth ongoing support, because I think each one of us would say that things that we learned [during the program] we've been able to take and apply to many other situations. So the impact of that work—just the twelve original of us—has had far-reaching effects.

Although the focus group interview offered the most robust articulation of PLS as beneficial professional development, individually the superintendents spoke to four aspects of PLS they found valuable as professional development. As Table 4.5 shows, two of the superintendents spoke to the value of a latecomer to the PLS teaching faculty, Brian Malt, who introduced to the group the value of role-playing simulations as a form of leadership team training. Three of the five spoke to the value of other PLS faculty as consultants to them in their individual districts and the implicit value of the process of presenting their own cases during the PLS sessions. Only one of the participants made specific remarks about the program as the source of a valuable network, although during the focus group interview the value of this network was more broadly articulated.

Table 4.5 PLS as Professional Development

Superintendent	Brian Malt's experiential teaching	Value of PLS faculty consultants	PLS case as valuable to learning	PLS as network
Maria			X	
Bobby			X	X
Tom	X	X	X	
Dee		X		
John	X	X		

Teaching Faculty, Faculty Consultants, and PLS Case Presentations as Critical Incidents

In the following section, I discuss other aspects of PLS that were deemed valuable components of PLS as professional development. While the program as a whole could be termed professional development or training (see Aguinis & Kraiger, 2009), the distinct categories outlined in Table 4.5 contributed to the unique design of PLS.

John and Tom spoke with varying degrees of appreciation for the work that Malt, an adjunct member of the PLS teaching team, brought to the overall value of the learning they gleaned from the teaching of adaptive leadership. Malt taught one full session of the program and presented the only formal simulation of the program. It consisted of a scripted dialogue between a superintendent, role-playing someone in a senior administrative position, and a direct report debriefing a meeting. This brief simulation created a moment of "difficult conversation" video-recorded and then played back to the entire group for comment. The felt value of this simulation as offering both emotional and cognitive kind of learning, and some of Malt's subsequent teaching around it, colored a memorable episode in the program that reverberated in certain of the superintendents' recollection of PLS.

This was an unexpected finding; I had not considered Malt's pedagogical teaching as a key element of PLS's curriculum, especially since it had been relatively brief in comparison to the amount of time the main PLS faculty spent teaching adaptive leadership concepts. To my surprise, Tom described teaching "a lot of Brian Malt" when creating curriculum for principals he taught in his current position as a professor. To a lesser extent, yet distinctly, John and Tom claimed to have valued Malt's experiential methods, such as role-playing a difficult conversation.

Another cluster of superintendents—Tom, Dee, and John—reported that they valued the faculty consultant assigned to them. These faculty consultants would work with the superintendents between formally convened sessions of PLS, both during in-person site visits to the superintendents' districts and on the phone.

Dee spoke at length about how Larry Sims helped her to see where different stakeholders in her community were perhaps coming from, and of how much she valued his input:

> [Larry] would oftentimes help me to stop and really look deeper into what they were trying to say; what the issue was. And I always really appreciated that. Because it would be easy just to go over something on the surface and take it for what it was. But he really helped me to see some other sides of folks or to at least consider what my thinking was about that; and, again, I think that was really helpful.

Tom and John spoke somewhat less extensively about their consultants; nonetheless, they remarked on their value in the program. As I have mentioned previously, Tom spent some time pointing out that one of the unique attributes of the design of PLS was that Foundation R. had allowed enough funding to provide for individual consultants for each of the participating superintendents.

Yet another configuration of superintendents—Maria, Bobby, and Tom—used the cases they had presented during PLS as critical incidents to describe their learning during the program. Maria and Bobby also made a point of mentioning how helpful it was to work in small groups on the cases they presented. As each case has been discussed earlier, they are given briefer treatment here.

The case Maria described that involved creating a new school in her district that would become a flagship technology-themed school, and her difficulty in dealing with the different factions of the community. A second case Maria presented in an ongoing way was that of the restructuring efforts under way in her district, and her changing role within that re-organization. Bobby's case concerned naming a school for a civil rights leader and (similarly to Maria's first case) negotiating a decision that worked for the community. Tom frequently returned to his case involving his desire to fire a deputy he perceived as incompetent and insubordinate, but whom he felt he could not fire for political reasons (Field notes, May 8, 2002; November 11, 2002; March 11, 2003; May 4, 2004).

While it may be argued that, in their recollection of their PLS experience, the superintendents naturally returned to cases they initially presented while the program was in session, it was my sense that these cases were brought up again in individual interviews because they had been more deeply processed during the earlier sessions. Thus, the value of having the case presentation method used during PLS is self-evident. Guilleux's (2011) discussion of case-in-point teaching underlines the effectiveness of this practice, a point that is supported by the literature (Levine, 2005; Parks, 2005).

For the purpose of group discussion during PLS sessions, each of the superintendents was asked to present a case of a leadership challenge they experienced. Maria remarked specifically and eloquently on the value of presenting the case studies. Speaking of the challenges faced when her district was undergoing a massive re-organization, she said,

> I actually remember the transition we were going through when . . . I was in the program, and I think that the support that I got from all of you in understanding . . . the case studies [presented during PLS sessions] . . . really [helped me in] trying to get a sense of my role and what was happening in [my district].

Summary of Section on PLS as Professional Development

All of the participating superintendents under discussion here found PLS to be a valuable learning experience. Not only was PLS beneficial in the realm of professional life, it was also seen by some as constructive in their personal life (as articulated by Tom). There was also evidence that the program challenged the superintendents in fresh ways, as it was deemed "unique" (as articulated by Maria and Dee).

Four distinct areas emerged as worthwhile components to PLS: the simulation exercise created by PLS faculty Brian Malt, the assigned faculty consultants, the use of personal case studies to present in session, and PLS as a valuable network. During the focus group interview, perhaps the most surprising finding to emerge was that at least one of the participating superintendents had lobbied Foundation R. to continue funding of PLS. From these interviews, I would conclude that the experimental nature of PLS (case presentations that asked the superintendents to address their failures instead of their successes; challenging of teaching style norms; simulations) proved most valuable to the superintendents. Across the cohort, superintendents seemed to have been most hungry for language with which to address their challenges. This language, in turn, in many cases led to adjustments in thinking and action. On those occasions where superintendents formed close ties with their faculty consultants, their learning was enhanced, and their actions modified.

Chapter Summary

This chapter has delineated the findings I have gathered through various data collection tools. The main tool used was that of the semi-structured interview with the PLS participants. I then organized the data into four broad domains:

1. The major challenges faced by the study sample superintendents
2. The major learning that occurred for the superintendents
3. To what extent transformative learning took place
4. PLS as professional development

The findings showed that superintendents each faced unique challenges, although the pool of challenges overlapped in different areas of their jobs. Many of them, for example, endured challenges with the boards to whom they reported. In terms of the learning of adaptive leadership concepts, these also overlapped, and the learning of adaptive leadership concepts was broad. Thus I have concluded from evidence in their testimony that superintendents also experienced transformative learning, but that this learning was only suggested, not definitive. Finally, the program was seen by participants as a valuable form of professional development, viewed for the most part as unlike any they had encountered.

The five major findings to emerge from the data were as follows:

1. School boards and politics of the community were most frequently cited as a problematic reality for superintendents in terms of the context in which they endeavored to apply concepts learned from PLS.
2. The contextual aspect of "getting to the balcony" seemed to affect the greatest number of superintendents in the ways in which they were able to newly perceive their jobs and their environment.
3. The concepts of Diagnosing Stakeholder Values, Managing Disequilibrium, and parsing the difference between Technical Work and Adaptive Work resonated the most for superintendents.
4. It was unclear that the superintendents had experienced transformative learning in a definitive way. Rather, indicators of changes in language and emotional cognizance, such as developing the ability to empathize with multiple viewpoints, including those that were dissonant with their own beliefs and values, were *suggestive* that transformative learning may have taken place.
5. The majority of superintendents saw PLS as a unique and highly valuable professional development vehicle.

Notes

1. See Heifetz (1994), who frequently uses "stew" as a metaphor regarding stakeholder values.
2. All of the superintendents I interviewed except Maria had a viable board; her district went through a restructuring process that so reduced the power of local school boards that the question in context did not really apply to her.
3. "Epistemic habits of mind relate to *the way we come to know things and the way we use that knowledge* [emphasis added]. Sociolinguistic perspectives are the way we view social norms, culture, and *how we use language* [emphasis added]. Psychological perspectives include our self-concept, personality, emotional responses, and personal images and dreams. Moral-ethical habits of mind incorporate our conscience and morality. Philosophical habits of mind are based on religious doctrine or world view. And our aesthetic habits of mind include our tastes and standards about beauty" (Cranton & Roy, 2003, p. 88).
4. The superintendents who are discussed here and who participated in the focus group interview were Maria, Bobby, Tom, and Dee.

References

Aguinis, H., & Kraiger, K. (2009). Benefits of training and development for individuals and teams, organizations, and society. *Annual Review of Psychology*, 60, 451–474.

Argyris, C. (1991). Teaching smart people how to learn. *Harvard Business Review*, 69(3).
Brookfield, S. (2000). Transformative learning as ideology critique. In J. Mezirow & Associates (Eds.), *Learning as transformation: Critical perspectives on a theory in progress* (pp. 125–148). San Francisco, CA: Jossey Bass.
Burke, W. W., Lake, D. G., & Paine, J. W. (2009). *Organization change: A comprehensive reader*. San Francisco, CA: Jossey Bass.
Cranton, P. A., & Roy, M. (2003). When the bottom falls out of the bucket: A holistic perspective on transformative learning. *Journal of Transformative Education*, 1(2), 86–98.
Drago-Severson, E. (2012). *Helping educators grow: Strategies and practices for leadership development*. Cambridge, MA: Harvard Education Press.
Elmore, R. F. (2000). *Building a new structure for school leadership*. Washington, DC: Albert Shanker Institute.
Erhard, W., Jensen, M. C., Zaffron, S., & Granger, K. L. (2012). *Creating leaders: An ontological/phenomenological model*. Working Paper. Harvard Business School Negotiations, Organizations and Markets Unit Research Paper Series No. 11-037; Barbados Group Working Paper No. 10-10; Simon School Working Paper No. FR-10-30. Retrieved from Social Sciences Research Network website: http://ssrn.com/abstract=1681682
Girczyc, P. A. (2008). *Toward a theory of intelligent leadership as adaptive action*. Doctoral dissertation. Retrieved from ProQuest Dissertations and Theses database.
Guilleux, F. (2011). *A developmental perspective on leadership education of aspiring principals*. Doctoral dissertation. Retrieved from ProQuest Dissertations and Theses database (UMI No. 3471901)
Heifetz, R. (1994). *Leadership without easy answers*. Cambridge, MA: Harvard University Press.
Heifetz, R., Grashow, A., & Linsky, M. (2009). *The practice of adaptive leadership: Tools and tactics for changing your organization and the world*. Cambridge, MA: Harvard Business School Press.
Heifetz, R., & Linsky, M. (2002). *Leadership on the line*. Cambridge, MA: Harvard Business School Press.
Levine, A. (2005). *Educating school leaders*. Washington, DC: Education Schools Project.
Mezirow, J. (1991). *Transformative dimensions of adult learning* (1st ed.). San Francisco, CA: Jossey Bass.
Mezirow, J. (2000). Learning to think like and adult: Core concepts of transformation theory. In J. Mezirow & Associates (Eds.), *Learning as transformation: Critical perspectives on a theory in progress* (pp. 3–33). San Francisco, CA: Jossey Bass.
Mezirow, J., & Associates. (2000). *Learning as transformation: Critical perspectives on a theory in progress*. San Francisco, CA: Jossey Bass.
Murphy, J. T. (1991). Superintendents as saviors: From the Terminator to Pogo. *Phi Delta Kappan*, 72, 507–513.
Okimoto, T. G., & Brescoll, V. L. (2010). The price of power: Power seeking and backlash against female politicians. *Personality and Social Psychology Bulletin*, 36(7), 923–936.
Parks, S. D. (2005). *Leadership can be taught: A bold approach for a complex world*. Cambridge, MA: Harvard Business School Press.
Salomon, G., & Perkins, D.N. (1989). Rocky roads to transfer: Rethinking mechanisms of a neglected phenomenon. *Educational Psychologist*, 24, 113–142.

Sandberg, S. (2013). *Lean in: Women, work, and the will to lead*. New York, NY: Knopf.

Starnes, B. (2011). Superstars, cheating and surprises. *Phi Delta Kappan*, 93(1). Retrieved from www.questia.com/library/journal/1G1-282444157/superstars-cheating-and-surprises

Yorks, L. (2003). Beyond the classroom: Transfer from work-based learning initiatives. In E. F. Holton & T. T. Baldwin (Eds.), *Improving learning transfer in organizations*. San Francisco, CA: Jossey Bass.

5 Sifting Through the Narrative

This study concerned the learning experienced by a small group of urban school superintendents, and the impact this learning had upon their practice as education professionals—both within their jobs as superintendents and beyond. Further, the study explored whether and how the superintendents were able to apply their learning in the context of their jobs. Finally, the study asked whether or not the superintendents who participated in PLS experienced Mezirow's model of transformative learning.

The primary methodology I employed to answer my research questions[1] was to conduct a series of semi-structured interviews with PLS participants. During these interviews, I asked the subjects for names of colleagues I could interview to give more texture to the research. Thus, my original study included learning experienced by superintendents and testimonies from their colleagues about any changes they observed in the superintendents during or after their participation in PLS. However, because of limitations imposed by guidelines protecting human subjects as outlined by the Institutional Review Board, I was unable to include the data from these interviews. I have also reviewed my own artifacts from the PLS program—data from field notes taken while managing the program and consulting to the teaching faculty of PLS.

The literature that has largely informed my study falls into three general areas: 1) the theory of adaptive leadership and the literature that forms its intellectual lineage, 2) an overview of preparation and training of school administrators, and 3) the adult education theory of transformative learning. As the scope of this book does not include a thorough literature review, I give it briefer treatment here, addressing the salient points of my survey.

Within the literature on education preparation of superintendents, an assertion is made by Murphy, Moorman, and McCarthy (2008) that a paradigmatic shift is needed in terms of how to properly educate and prepare school administrators. This shift needs to move from "the bridge metaphor" of teaching theory that informs practice—in other words, "bridging" theory to practice through application of theory—to the more complex metaphor of a "new design that looks more like a strand of DNA, where knowledge and practice are integrally intertwined" (p. 2195).

The notion of intertwining knowledge and practice forms a thread across the three areas of the literature. Adaptive leadership, as taught in PLS and elsewhere, involves case-in-point teaching, where the cases of the participants are used as data for interpretation through the concepts of adaptive leadership (Parks, 2005). A theme of the general failure to provide adequate preparation for school superintendents concerns the failure of knowledge imparted through training and educational preparation in order to meet the needs of practice (Levine, 2005). Finally, there is the notion of intertwining self-knowledge with action, which is seen in Mezirow's construct of transformative learning and which asserts that the re-conceptualization of one's self through the integration of new ways of being occurs upon the expansion or the discarding of assumptions. Additional literature informs this chapter in analyzing the data—that of transfer of training, as well as that of linguistics. I use this literature as a lens through which to analyze the reported effects of PLS and to inform recommendations for future research.

This chapter analyzes and interprets the main findings from this study.

Main Findings

As discussed in the last chapter, the main findings of this study are as follows:

1. School boards and politics of the community were most frequently cited as a problematic reality for superintendents in terms of the context in which they endeavored to apply concepts learned from PLS.
2. The contextual aspect of "getting to the balcony" seemed to affect the greatest number of superintendents in the ways in which they were able to newly perceive their jobs and their environment.
3. The concepts of Diagnosing Stakeholder Values, Managing Disequilibrium, and parsing the difference between Technical Work and Adaptive Work resonated the most for superintendents.
4. Indicators of changes in language and emotional cognizance, such as increased empathy, were suggestive that transformative learning may have taken place.
5. The majority of superintendents saw PLS as a unique and highly valuable professional development vehicle.

Table 5.1 provides a summary of changes reported by the participants, changes they attributed in whole or in part to their learning from PLS. The first column of this table summarizes the change undergone by the superintendent. The second column provides an example from the superintendent's interview with me.

As the table demonstrates, each of the PLS superintendents reported at least one concrete change as a result of participating in the program. These changes varied in specificity of reporting, although they were all

92   *Sifting Through the Narrative*

Table 5.1 Summary of Changes Reported by Superintendents as a Result of Learning

Superintendent	Reported Change/Effect of PLS	Example(s)
Maria	Increased empathy for adversaries	Coping with board members
Maria	Recognition of role as lightning rod	Awareness of holding colleagues through the restructuring changes in her district
Bobby	Increased ability to give work back to the group and not always be "the answer guy"	Allowing teachers to propose a school merger and allowing process to unfold
Tom	Increased interest in using experiential learning for professional development of staff and teaching	Sent a principal to a highly experiential program to improve principal's performance
John	Increased awareness of the "dynamic tensions" in a system	Used metaphor of turning up the heat in the system to increase or decrease pressure "to move the system"
Dee	Increased awareness of values others held	Partnering with representatives of African American community during a hiring decision for a new principal
Dee	Increased curiosity about how perceived	Asked faculty consultant to conduct interviews with her peers so as to gain knowledge of how she was perceived

connected with work superintendents undertook in their districts, either during or subsequent to participation in PLS. Maria's reporting was perhaps the most amorphous, as she described her level of awareness increasing around the values her adversaries held and the pain her colleagues went through during a restructuring process.

Analyzing and Interpreting Adaptive Leadership Concepts Learned During PLS

The first of the major findings relates to Research Question 1: What did the superintendents learn in PLS and how did they learn it? The discoveries made through the data collection relate more to the first part of this question than the second. The superintendents clearly learned a number of adaptive leadership concepts from PLS. What was less clear is exactly *how* they learned them. One might speculate that applying a conceptual lens in order to articulate their challenges, such as articulating a challenge or a problematic reality as being "technical work" or "adaptive work," is the "how" of their learning.

Learning Transfer

Holton and Baldwin (2003) define the "distance" of learning transfer as the level of abstraction or complexity to which training is transferred. In a highly technical training, such as learning to drive a car, the transition or "transfer" from driving a car to driving a small truck would be a "short distance." Conversely, the learning of complex management theory and attempting a departmental re-organization, for example, would be an example of a learning transfer of "much greater distance" (pp. 7–8). These analogies are useful for understanding the learning and "transfer" of learning that occurred for the PLS superintendents. Mere adaptation of language and establishment of study groups among one's staff would imply "short distance" learning. Endeavoring to shift the values of a system, such as John undertook when he spoke of "turning up the heat" in County K. by introducing an International Baccalaureate program, implies "greater distance." Another way of stating these ideas is "low-road" (short distance) and "high-road" (greater distance) transfer (see Salomon & Perkins, 1989, as cited in Yorks, 2003).

While adaptive leadership concepts have been discussed extensively, the essence of the theory informing adaptive leadership lies with the challenge of shifting values, beliefs, perceptions, and assumptions (Heifetz, Grashow, & Linsky 2009). One question for analysis, then, is as follows: Did participants in PLS *engage in* adaptive leadership as well as learn *about* it? Again, this question relates to "low-road transfer" and "high-road" transfer. As Erhard, Jensen, Zaffron, and Granger (2012), in their own very similar model of leadership teaching, put it: Were the participants in this program learning leadership ontologically, in the sense of *being* leaders or (put another way) "exercising leadership"—or were they merely engaged in learning about various phenomena, for which they learned a kind of vocabulary (p. 2)? Data collected from the interviews conducted for this study demonstrate that, for the most part, PLS participants learned the concepts of adaptive leadership on an ontological or "being" level. Thus the degree to which they learned this on a "being" level determined the potential depth of their transformative learning, as well as whether these were "low-" or "high-road" transfers of learning.

That 100% of the superintendents could relate to and apply the concepts of Diagnosing Stakeholder Values and Managing Disequilibrium reflects the condition of such urban school superintendents during what Hess (1999) has referred to as a situation of "spinning wheels" (in the

94 *Sifting Through the Narrative*

sense of a car being stuck in the mud). This metaphor for education reform pervades the education landscape in the US, particularly in urban districts. Similar to Murphy et al. (2008), Hess uses the image of "churning" to express the constant policy shifts around reform in urban school districts. Hess also alludes to the political nature of urban school districts, where reform is part of the unconscious politics of a community (p. 4). The notion that reform is part of the "unconsciousness" of such politics is likely a contributing factor to the confusion faced by urban school superintendents. It would account for the PLS cohort's particular resonance with the idea of how to Diagnose Stakeholder Values as a way to put order into the chaotic situations of their communities by surfacing certain dynamics and, in so doing, dispelling the "unconsciousness" of such forces. As Hess describes the general situation in urban school districts:

> The problem is not that districts do a number of things.... The problem is that urban districts appear to do a number of things in a stop-and-start, chaotic fashion that is not part of any clear strategy to improve specific elements of school performance.
>
> (p. 8)

While this study did not address issues of education reform as such, the pervasiveness of the reform movement in education has not abated between the time of Hess's study of 57 urban districts and that of my interviews with this group of superintendents approximately one decade later. In other words, not much has changed over the years in terms of education reform being a source of overwhelm for superintendents.

The PLS superintendents may have resonated strongly with notions of Managing Disequilibrium and Diagnosing Stakeholder Values because these terms articulated and seemed to clarify the politics with which they were contending. As I have stated previously, the impetus for Foundation R.'s underwriting the grant for PLS was to assist them in their political leadership skills. The teaching of such leadership skills was seen by the foundation as largely absent in the training and preparation of school superintendents. The differing demographics (e.g., age, level of education, number of years in the superintendency) of these superintendents (while attending PLS) reflect the demographics of urban superintendents throughout the US and thus imply that their needs are reflective of those among most urban superintendents for this kind of political training (Grogan, 2000). While it would be inappropriate for me to make a sweeping generalization about superintendents based on the small group that comprised my study, the need for political training could probably be generalized to many, if not most, superintendents.

Across the interviews the superintendents alluded to Managing Disequilibrium by attempting to understand the values of different

Table 5.2 Analysis of Superintendents' Departures From Districts

Superintendent	Left under negative circumstances	Left under positive/neutral circumstance	Demonstrated capacity to manage disequilibrium through empathizing with adversaries
Maria		X	X
Bobby		X	
Tom	X		
Dee		X	X
John	X		X

stakeholders in the system, yet half of them were successful in managing disequilibrium and half were seemingly unable to do so. Here I have used data gleaned on how PLS superintendents departed from the districts they led during the time of PLS. Table 5.2 outlines my analysis of the mode in which superintendents left their PLS districts and their demonstrated learning around Managing Disequilibrium.

Tom and John departed from their districts somewhat involuntarily, or "under a cloud," while Maria, Bobby, and Dee appear to have endured far less controversy when they stepped down. Data from the interviews with the superintendents who left "under a cloud," however, show only slightly less capacity to Diagnose Stakeholder Values in a positive light than do the data for those superintendents who left their districts without controversy. John, for example, spoke of understanding (in a largely empathic way) the reasons the state-imposed control board would have wanted to replace him, even though his local board did not. And while Maria demonstrated a capacity to empathize with those stakeholders in her district with whom she disagreed, Bobby appeared to be considerably less empathic with factions in his community who argued against equity for all students. My conclusion, then, is that having the perspicacity to Diagnose Stakeholder Values, even empathically, does not necessarily lead to a successful management of disequilibrium.

Race

Other factors may have contributed to why these superintendents left under less than favorable circumstances, and these have to do with external circumstances, elements more distal to PLS, such as the shifting demographics and political compositions of districts.

In the cases of the two superintendents who left under a cloud—both of whom were white males—the demographic data of their districts may also have been a factor in the politics of their districts. While the data for the poverty index in Tom's district were unavailable for the years in which he was superintendent, recent reports indicated at least 25% of the population in his district living in poverty. During the time of Tom's participation in PLS, nearly half of the students in his district were children of color. In John's district, nearly three-quarters of the student population were eligible for free and reduced lunch, and close to 80% of the population were people of color. As Tom reported in his interview, he had a keen awareness of his political disadvantage as "a white guy" in a largely African American city. And John was quite candid in his perceptions that a key factor in the political forces instrumental in forcing a resignation decision had to do with the desire for a non-white superintendent to take his place.

In this small study sample, therefore, the two white males in the cohort felt that race was a distinct political factor in their districts. This leads me to speculate that these dynamics are reflective of the racial tensions in the US that continue to be problematic. As Charles Blow wrote in a column for the *New York Times* with regard to the infamous case of Trayvon Martin, an unarmed black teenager shot by a neighborhood watch individual in Florida who was armed,

> The system failed [Martin] when . . . [the man who shot him, George Zimmerman] grafted on stereotypes the moment he saw [Martin], ascribing motive and behavior and intent and criminal history to a boy who was just walking home.
>
> (2013)

Since then, of course, we have seen the rise of videotaped acts of heinous aggression on the part of white police officers toward black men (and, occasionally, black women). The Black Lives Matter movement has coalesced around this systemic failure and may be analyzed through the lens of group relations (cf. Chace, 2017). The racial inequalities and prejudices abiding in the US justice system are symptomatic of the other forces at play in American society when it comes to race. Whether conscious or unconscious in the politics of the superintendents' communities, these forces were part of what the superintendents both embodied and contended with.

Coping with Factions

In coping with factions, the findings also suggest that learning to Diagnose Stakeholder Values was helpful to superintendents in understanding their jobs and in making the politics of their communities more "conscious" (to use Hess's word) for the superintendents. Dee provided a summary that spoke to the prominence of this concept among the PLS cohort:

So [I benefited from learning concepts from] . . . the Adaptive Work in general; but [the] one in particular I really do stop and pause about often, and really think about [is]: Who people are working with, what their agenda is; understanding that people have agendas that they have to be true to also and just trying to be able to work with them deeply and not just on the surface; all that kind of thing.

The findings for Managing Disequilibrium (in the sense of becoming adept at Diagnosing Stakeholder Values by, for example, forging relationships with a diverse community) are further verified by Remland's 2012 study of factors that led to the longevity of superintendency in an urban school district in California. According to Remland, a "prominent" skill that accounts for the success of superintendents in this urban area was "an ability to develop strategic and authentic relationships" (p. 68). This skill suggests that an understanding of and appreciation for stakeholder values would likely contribute to an urban school superintendent's longevity.

Managing Disequilibrium, in the sense of trying to either produce more "heat" in a system or to turn the "temperature" down by, for example, putting pressure on teachers to learn and teach a curriculum for the International Baccalaureate or, conversely, tamp down anxieties about school mergers, was also a powerful metaphor for the superintendents in terms of providing an articulation for the dynamics of their communities. And while all of the superintendents appeared to resonate with this term to a greater or lesser extent, John and Tom emerged as most interested in "turning up the heat" in their districts. All three spoke to me about what John termed "dynamic tension" in the system of a school district, and the need to keep the tension heightened in order for progress to be made. Tom spoke of this mostly in terms of orchestrating conflict in a general sense, and in being aware that he needed to surround himself with deputies who were more cautious than he. John alluded most specifically to a need to increase the pressure on his then-current district (County K.) by creating an International Baccalaureate program at the high school. The remainder of the PLS cohort under discussion here—Maria, Bobby, and Dee—seemed to feel a need to keep the "heat" of the disequilibrium in their districts tamped down. In other words, they were more aware of the dangers of having too much heat in the system rather than too little.

Yet the notion of Managing Disequilibrium, while a powerful image for all of the PLS superintendents, did not necessarily engender the actual capacity to carry it out, particularly when the superintendent's inclination was to "turn the heat up." John's portrayal of District S. as a place where one person's gain became another's loss describes a system where the disequilibrium was difficult to manage, and he seemed to have had little control over the "temperature" in this system. In one case, however, a superintendent was more successful. In a detailed account of disequilibrium managed successfully, Dee described the process she went through when she decided not to hire an African American male for a principal position in her district. By zeroing in on the values of key stakeholders embodied in the opinion of a local NAACP representative, Dee recalled that this act of partnering was "the right thing to do." The "right thing to do," in this case, could be read as knowing how to keep the heat engendered by potential controversy at a tolerable level for the community. However, the difference between the level of volatility in John's and Dee's districts should be taken into account. It is certainly easier to disturb a system that has less turbulence in it to begin with.

Although a universal appreciation prevailed among the PLS cohort for the concepts of Diagnosing Stakeholder Values and Managing Disequilibrium, within this universality there appeared to be a racial dimension to the ways in which superintendents of color managed their jobs. Those who left their superintendencies "under a cloud" were both Caucasian (John and Tom). When looking at 20th-century traditions of superintendencies as being held by white male "pillars of society" (Glass, Bjork, & Brunner, 2000; Grogan, 2000), it may seem surprising that it was the two white males who had the most difficulty in their districts. And yet the emerging paradigm of the 21st century contains within it the assumption that communities and those authority figures who are in charge of them will be increasingly racially diverse. It is reasonable to speculate, then, that at least part of the problem faced by John and Tom was that their disruptive ideas were less likely to be tolerated than they might have been in an earlier era. As Ortiz and Ortiz (1995) wrote over 20 years ago: "Educational administration practice as it is presently conducted is directly lodged on the knowledge base formulated by and for white males" (p. 158). This assertion is no longer necessarily true. The changing demographics of urban areas may, in the first decade of the 21st century, have made it more difficult for white male superintendents to "turn up the heat" where racial tensions exist. As previously discussed, demographics may have played a substantial role in the demise of their PLS superintendencies.

Conversely, one trend I observed in the PLS cohort might indicate a possibility that minority superintendents are better overall at managing disequilibrium—disequilibrium that otherwise might cause their professional undoing. In a 2006 study, Johnson found that female African American superintendents emerged as both "tempered radicals" (Meyerson, 2001) and "servant leaders" (Greenleaf, 1977). It would appear that Bobby's approach to his superintendency were those of a tempered radical, while Maria's approach would fit Greenleaf's definition of servant leadership. As Johnson (p. 148), citing Greenleaf (1977), describes characteristics of servant leadership, these have included "empathy . . . awareness . . .

[and] healing." A "tempered radical" will "rock the boat and stay in the boat" (Meyerson, 2001, p. xi). I would interpret both Bobby's view of how to manage his job as that of a tempered radical, as a substantial portion of his being focused on the need to keep the distress of closing schools within a realm of manageability.

I would also compare the findings from Johnson's study with Maria's openness to applying new concepts when under pressure in her district—a sign of her tendencies toward servant leadership. While Maria self-identified as Hispanic and not as African American, it seemed clear from Maria's interview (as well as from my own observations of her for the duration of the program) that she was a person of "empathy," "awareness," and "healing" (see Greenleaf, 1977, op. cit.). As Maria's greatest learning seems to have been around enhancing an already empathic *modus operandi*, her application of PLS concepts within her context closely resembled the conclusions drawn by Johnson about African American female superintendents—i.e., that a component of servant leadership became a part of her general approach.

Another aspect of Maria's talent for managing disequilibrium in enormously complex circumstances is reflected and articulated in Torres's 2004 study of Hispanic female urban school superintendents. Torres invokes the notion of a "balancing act," an image that echoes Maria's own image of "walking the tightrope" as she handled her district during a time of high distress. Among Torres's findings, in a study examining six female Hispanic superintendents in New York City, was the sense on the part of participants that they "felt they were hired to 'fix' the district and resolve a myriad of issues" (p. 199). A successful candidate for hire would likely be one who was good at managing disequilibrium and understanding stakeholder values.

In addition, the universal application of the new language of "technical work" versus "adaptive work," while not verbalized extensively by the superintendents during their interviews, was nonetheless assimilated by them. Each of the superintendents, whether explicitly or implicitly, mentioned these terms. In a 2004 article that appeared in the journal *Educational Leadership*, Heifetz and Linsky diagnose a failure of leadership on the part of a district superintendent who "solves" the problem of an "abrasive principal" about whom teachers lodged complaints. The superintendent, in this case, "found a way to promote the principal out of her job" (Heifetz & Linsky, 2004, p. 34). In exercising leadership, this was a failed solution, one in which the technical work of removing the principal failed to address the adaptive challenge of helping teachers cope with being pushed beyond their comfort zones, or what they perceived as beyond their capacity. Such a case would be defined as a misdiagnosis, using a technical solution to solve an adaptive problem, and a common one among groups and organizations. It also exemplifies a situation in which a district superintendent chose to keep the heat turned

100   *Sifting Through the Narrative*

down, thereby "managing disequilibrium" engendered by the teachers' complaints. In this situation, as in so many others, the overlap among all three of the concepts (diagnosing stakeholder values, managing disequilibrium, and discriminating between technical and adaptive work) with which the superintendents resonated is evident and understandable. In order to manage disequilibrium, the PLS superintendents at times sought to empathize with stakeholder values. In order to more finely calibrate the sources of the disequilibrium and the most efficacious solutions to these problems, superintendents in this study sought to define them as either technical or adaptive.

Uses of Language: Games

The employment of certain terms to articulate circumstances or situations is analogous to linguistic theory about games (cf. Harris, 1990). The words "technical" and "adaptive" might mean many things to different sorts of people within their context. Technical manuals, for instance, connote a specific meaning. Technical writing is a profession. To be a technician in one field (for instance, the medical field) is different from being a technician in another (e.g., an aircraft). Similarly, *adaptation* or *to be adaptive* connotes a number of different meanings. Darwin, who inspired Heifetz's conception of adaptive leadership, describes the evolution of species on the physical plane, while Heifetz extrapolates the notion of adaptation to environment in terms of psychic, political, and emotional forces. Thus, we have what Saussure and Wittgenstein might describe as a "game" around language. As Harris has summarized this idea, words must be seen in context, just as chess pieces must be used in the context of the rules of the game (p. 25).

Analyzing and Interpreting Findings Related to Context

The second major finding to emerge from this study demonstrates how the greatest problematic realities for this elite sample were consistent with the research on superintendents, particularly urban school superintendents. This finding relates to Research Question 2: In what ways were superintendents able to apply concepts learned in PLS in the context of their jobs? What follows emphasizes the context of jobs—i.e., the most vividly articulated aspects of their jobs—and their attendant challenges. The "context," here, is defined as the politics of the school board and the local politics of the community consistently posed the greatest challenges for the superintendents.

Here I have chosen to analyze this portion of the findings in "group-analytic" terms, specifically focusing on the phenomenon called "parallel process," wherein what happens in the smaller group may resonate with dynamics in the larger group. As discussed in Chapter 3, parallel process has been studied empirically to prove that the smaller system will contain the larger in much the same way a cell contains a strand of the DNA for a given organism. Like a recognizable quote from a play, the information may be incomplete, but it will be recognizable (R. Garisto, personal communication, August 11, 2017). Similarly, Elmore (2000) describes the phenomenon of politics of the community as closely linked with the politics of the school board:

> Local politics is usually driven by pluralist imperatives; local factions mobilize by neighborhood, by racial or ethnic group, or by moral principle, they galvanize electoral support, and they reproduce, not surprisingly, the same political divisions on school boards as exist in the community at large.
>
> (pp. 7–8)

Such a situation as described by Elmore is germane to findings for this study. In interviews with each of the PLS superintendents, stories were told about challenges with the board and with the community. In many cases, these challenges were difficult to tease apart. Maria's case of creating a new "flagship" school in her district was representative of how the challenges of community and board seemed to blend:

[T]he Board members who were representing the minority community ([i.e.,] the Hispanic and African American [community]) felt that they were being excluded . . . from [another] high school [when we created a new one in the district]. And my position was: "Look . . . you're still going to have access and . . . X number of students still have access to the school. In addition, too, there's a lottery system."

> And so what I proposed to the community was we're going to make this like a flagship school. . . . And so I believe it was a win/win for both communities. Of course, there are different perspectives . . . in how board members may have perceived it. But I think in the end it was a good resolution.

In terms of the "petri dish" of local politics, as mirrored in the relationship of the superintendent to the board, those superintendents who gave the most detailed accounts of their successes in the community were also those who seemed least troubled by their boards: Bobby and Dee. Even in the focus group interview, where the superintendents seemed to enjoy talking more to one another than to me—and were, in this group interview, presumably even more candid than in their individual interviews—the "evil" nature of the school board was tempered by Bobby's characterization of these local governing entities as being "challenging." And while Dee, for the most part, led the discussion overall, during the focus group interview, she did not lead the discussion about the boards, which was led by others, with Maria weighing in on the positive effects of school boards being eliminated in favor of mayoral control within her district.

Of additional interest to me is the fact that the two superintendents who seemed to have coped most successfully with potentially explosive community challenges, were Bobby and Dee, both of whose professional lives seemed to align with the human relations aspects of their jobs. Bobby spent much of his pre-superintendent career as a human resources professional, and Dee held 18 different positions in her district prior to becoming superintendent, a variety of experience that presumably gave her a fairly comprehensive view of the district she eventually came to serve as superintendent. This affiliation with human relations *cum* human resources, suggests that both Bobby and Dee were versatile in their "people skills," which may have accounted for their capacity to cope with disparate elements in their communities. This analysis is consistent with Grogan's research (2000), which asserts that contemporary superintendents' jobs have a "heightened need for finely tuned human relations skills, ones that allow superintendents to understand the diverse and often divisive groups they serve" (p. 118).

Across interviews, and in the literature at large, the micro-management on the part of school boards is often seen as a problem. The superintendents who alluded to this were John and Tom. John's interview is representative: "The board got into a very much hands-on mode of being involved with all kinds of minutiae decision-making stuff in the system and so I've had to back them off from that and try to establish CEO control." Again, the superintendents who mentioned boards' micro-management as problematic were either fired or more or less forced out of their positions at some point in their career as superintendents. Maria, Bobby, and Dee did not mention school boards as acutely problematic (though all of the superintendents acknowledged that the structural existence of school boards was at least somewhat problematic). In contrast to John and Tom, these three superintendents did not report having left their superintendent positions involuntarily or even under "cloudy" circumstances.

Much of the literature around education reform has been consistent in articulating the idea of the school board being outdated, particularly in an urban setting. As noted earlier, Maria spoke of the situation in her large and complex city as "better" with the elimination of school boards. The literature also indicates, however, that the elimination of school boards in favor of mayoral control might simply be a "technical fix" for an "adaptive challenge." Hess (2010) has cautioned against the magical thinking of mayoral control as the "silver bullet" for managing districts, while at the same time he acknowledges that "troubled" urban districts may benefit from executive centralization. The deeper problem, however, lies with the structure of the school district itself, says Hess—an assertion that seems to reify the notion of the smaller group's (i.e., the board's) dysfunctions as a reflection of the larger systemic challenges. This reification perhaps reflects society's inability to cope with complex education challenges (see National Center for Education and the Economy report, 2007).

Images of the Job

The third major finding for this study also derives from Research Question 2—the part of the question that asks, "*In what ways* [emphasis added] were superintendents able to apply concepts learned in PLS?" All of the superintendents here discussed testified to a new understanding of their jobs after applying the adaptive leadership concepts learned in PLS to their contexts. More importantly, I noticed evidence of the cohort's newly perceived image and understanding of how to operate in their jobs.

I use the phrase "newly perceived image" as a paraphrase for the non-therapeutic sense of the word *gestalt*. The sense in which I use this term is articulated in the leadership literature, broadly speaking. Specifically, Jim Collins' prescription for taking a business "from good to great" offers a scenario of transition; Collins invokes the word "gestalt" as I mean to use it in this context:

> We must think of transition as a process followed by breakthrough, broken into three stages: disciplined people, disciplined thought, and disciplined action. Within each of these three stages, there are two concepts: the buildup and the breakthrough. . . . Wrapping around the entire framework is a concept called the flywheel, which captures the *gestalt* of the entire process of going from good to great.
> (Collins, 2001, p. 14, emphasis added)

While this study was not asking the question of how to go "from good to great," it did ask if A led to B—i.e., did participating in PLS lead to changes in how superintendents conceived of operating in their districts? The salient finding for this part of the study's inquiry is that the learning from PLS was applied in the context of participants' jobs, with the most pronounced results occurring as a change in how superintendents experienced the gestalt of their jobs.

As a result of their learning, superintendents seemed to feel less that they had to be, in Bobby's words, "the answer guy," and more able to ask questions of themselves and of their teams. In the language of the transfer of training literature, "Q learning" seems to have occurred (Revans, 1982, 1989, as cited in Yorks, 2003, p. 145). "Q learning" refers to the ability to formulate what Revans calls "questioning insight" or what "Pedler (1991) refers to . . . as asking discriminating questions." More simply put, Q learning is "a change in how one interprets a situation" (Yorks, 2003, p. 151).

Overall, the superintendents were more willing to explore new ways of operating in their districts as a result of their learning. Both Maria and Dee considered PLS "perfect timing" for where they were in their careers. And in an example of seeking to discern a gestalt on her presence in the district, Dee described how she employed her faculty consultant, Larry, to get a more objective view of herself and how she was seen in her district.

This finding on how superintendents perceived their jobs as a result of their learning aligns with those of Roughton's 2007 study of the importance of "the first 90 days" of a superintendent's orientation to a new job in a district. In this study, "Participants reported that they were unprepared for the political aspect of the superintendency" (p. 1). Roughton reinforces the idea that a new concept of the superintendency as an overwhelmingly political job might help superintendents envision a more precise and pragmatic image of their jobs from the outset. This would be especially true for those education administrators who emerged from a traditional vertical climb up the ladder of an education career. Burry's 2003 study points to the multiple and shifting roles of an urban school superintendent as indicative of Kuhn's notion of paradigm shift (Kuhn, 1970). Burry has placed the situation of the urban school superintendent, a place close to crisis, as indicative of such a shift. This situating of the blurred role of a superintendent is by definition confusing. And yet, as Jentz and Murphy (2005) assert, "embracing confusion," is, paradoxically, the way out of confusion. Creating a gestalt of their own, Jentz and Murphy offer advice for anyone in a leadership position, including urban school superintendents:

> Being confused ... does not mean being incapacitated. Indeed, one of the most liberating truths of leadership is that confusion is not quicksand from which to escape but rather the potter's clay of leadership—the very stuff with which managers work.
>
> (p. 366)

My own interpretation of a gestalt shift, on the part of the PLS superintendents, is that they were, for the most part, able to see anew their challenges as "clay," rather than "quicksand," through the application of adaptive leadership concepts learned in PLS and re-conceptualize themselves and their contexts as a result.

Transformative Learning

The final research question informing this study asked whether and if transformative learning was engendered for superintendents participating in PLS. The main finding for this question, which relates to Research Question 3 ("In what ways [if any] was learning of PLS concepts similar to [or did it engender] transformative learning?"), is that, within the domains of communicative learning, superintendents may have experienced transformative learning as they underwent perspective shifts. A shift in language, in and of itself, does not necessarily equal a shift in behavior or in meaning-making; however, in this section, I will discuss the kinds of shifts undergone by superintendents.

The main finding for this portion of the study shows that participating superintendents by and large experienced at least the suggestion of a shift in perspective socio-linguistically. Such a finding is not surprising, given the confusion that seems to pervade the experience of urban school superintendents. The state of confusion and, often, frustration that pervade the world of a superintendent would, in my view, make the desire increasingly acute for a new way of learning and articulating their challenges.

Sociolinguistic shifts in perspective, although not necessarily indicative of definitive transformative learning, are reminiscent of literary theory's "linguistic revolution," which focuses on the notion of language as the engine for meaning-making. Eagleton (1983) writes that

> The hallmark of the "linguistic revolution" of the twentieth century, from Saussure to Wittgenstein to contemporary literary theory, is the recognition that meaning is not simply something "expressed" or "reflected" in language: it is actually *produced* by it [emphasis in the original]. It is not as though we have meanings, or experiences, which we then proceed to cloak with words; we can only have the meanings and experiences in the first place because we have a language to have them in.
>
> (p. 60)

The sociolinguistic turn in the superintendents' learning seems to have taken hold because the superintendents now had language, or diagnostic terms, via which to "produce" the meaning they made of their experiences.

The theory underlying transformative learning is based on sociology; however, the aspect of perspective shift residing in sociolinguistic learning has inspired me to consider the work of literary theorists when examining the superintendents' employment of adaptive leadership's conceptual terms to articulate their challenges and strategies. Literary theory provides a focus on the place of language in terms of the meaning-making germane to this study. While Cranton and Roy (2003) have parsed Mezirow's theory in terms of sociolinguistic transformative learning, embedded in that parsing is connective tissue to Saussure's semiotics, or the notion of "signifier" and "signified," where, for example, the letters "c-a-t" refer, as Eagleton says (invoking Saussure), to "the real furry four-legged creature" (1983, pp. 96–97). Similarly, though much more broadly, through the invention of diagnostic terms such as "technical work" and "adaptive work," Heifetz's adaptive leadership has created linguistic signifiers for certain kinds of "problematizing" (Freire, 1970)—the excavation of a problematic reality having to do with "one's being and role in the world" (Montero, 2011)—such as the technical fix of removing a principal from her job in order to tamp down teacher complaints, rather than the unearthing of the adaptive challenge indicated by the complaints (Heifetz & Linsky, 2004).

As discussed in Chapter 4, I found that the majority of the superintendents used precise terms from adaptive leadership in their interviews. In fact, Maria used the term "disequilibrium" and "adaptive change" when speaking of Heifetz's influence on her work, and these terms are closely associated with notions of "adaptive leadership," "adaptive challenge," and "managing disequilibrium."

It is worth noting that the language of adaptive leadership also provides a sense of belonging. The terms associated with adaptive leadership—technical vs. adaptive work, managing disequilibrium, Diagnosing Stakeholder Values via the "pizza diagrams"—provide a kind of binding for any group engaged in learning adaptive leadership. To make an unlikely comparison, those who employ the terms of adaptive leadership could be compared to a sort of gang, whose uses of language denote a code (cf. Labov, 1972). Just as inner-city youth from troubled homes may join a gang to give them a sense of place, family, and even safety, the language of adaptive leadership for this group of urban school superintendents gave them a sense of belongingness. The disequilibrium of a broken education system may heighten a comparable sense, on the part of urban school superintendents, to look for a place where they belong and feel understood.

In conclusion, I have arrived at the belief that the function of language itself is a key component in teaching adaptive leadership. The lack of clarity that may accompany a constant state of disequilibrium, and a shifting of paradigms that exists in urban school districts, may have ripened the moment (Heifetz, 1994) for a new language to articulate the challenges of the superintendency shared by this unique cohort. Adaptive leadership terms such as "technical work," "adaptive challenges," "getting to the balcony," and "distributing loss at a rate the group can tolerate," may someday become common language for superintendents.

PLS as Professional Development

The final piece of analysis for this study concerns how I have come to view PLS as a professional development program. This portion of the analysis of findings forms a connective tissue among the three research questions informing this study. It encompasses the findings related to adaptive leadership concepts that were learned, the context in which they were applied (which is the salient purpose of professional development), and it examines transformative learning through the lens of transfer of training.

In Teitel's 2006 report, a series of "snapshot" descriptions emerged through "snowball" sampling of superintendent professional development programs. These programs, like PLS, were created for sitting superintendents (Teitel, 2005, 2006). One finding to emerge from this exploration that involved a variety of professional development programs was the need for a "safe space" in which to convene so as to discuss common challenges. This finding is consistent with Orr's study on preparation programs for superintendents (2006). Other findings from Teitel's report imply that, as professional development, PLS contained commonalities with the programs he examined (Teitel, 2006, p. 1). For example, the superintendents interviewed by Teitel valued "peers and fellow participants whom they respect and can build relationships with" (p. 5). This phrase could summarize the tenor of the conversation in my own study's focus group, as well as the recollections of the superintendents about their learning while PLS was in session. Teitel's additional findings could also describe PLS—e.g., the value of "personal learning about one's own leadership" and "practical and useful ideas that connect to their work in their districts" (p. 5). Similarly to Murphy et al. (2008), Helsing, Howell, Kegan, and Lahey (2008), Guilleux (2011), and Drago-Severson (2012), Teitel also uses "technical" and "adaptive" terminology to limn the nature of the superintendents' work. "Whether the focus is on immediate technical skills or long-term adaptive growth, a key element [of these programs] has been connecting to, and having an impact on, the school district of the superintendent" (p. 5).

Drago-Severson's 2012 book, *Helping Educators Grow*, describes classes and workshops similar to PLS, citing the importance of trust and safety (p. 49) for optimal learning to take place. While issues of trust and safety were not specifically explored in this study, the importance of these components cannot be overlooked when considering the exposure and vulnerability most urban superintendents endure. The components of trust and safety allowed the PLS superintendents to discuss their dilemmas freely with one another, in both small- and large-group discussions, and perhaps provided them with their most memorable learning. Drago-Severson's longitudinal study on the learning students most remembered—from a graduate course she taught on leadership for educators—revealed a finding that supports the findings for this study. Referring to her former graduate students, "who are now school leaders and education leadership university professors" as remembering "the class as a holding environment," Drago-Serverson reported that "many [of her former students] said that they felt they were able to grow from experiencing the class and can now better assist in supporting the growth of adults with whom they work" (p. 49). This finding reflects a similar picture of PLS superintendents sharing their learning with their own staffs and replicating some of the materials and methods used in PLS.

While the study found within these pages was not conceived as an evaluation of a professional development program, as a case study, it has attempted to capture the effects of learning from a leadership training program on practice.

Guilleux, for example, conducted a study resembling this one, examining the learning of a group of school principals who underwent a preparatory leadership training program using case-in-point teaching methods of adaptive leadership (cf. Parks, 2005). When developing the research questions for his study, Guilleux employed Kegan's constructive-developmental theory as a framing device for the principals' learning, and posed a question echoed by this study: "In what ways, if any, does case-in-point teaching support shifts in perspective-taking?" (Guilleux, 2011, p. 8). He also integrated Mezirow with Kegan (p. 37) and offered an integrated frame through which to sift the data of his participants' learning. In such a pedagogy, Kegan would occupy a place concerned with creating a holding environment for the case-in-point teaching method "by offering supports and challenges that are developmentally appropriate to the *different ways in which we each make sense of experiences* (i.e., ways of knowing)" (Drago-Severson, 2012, p. 47, emphasis in the original). The developmental level at which an adult finds herself making sense of the world is a central component of Kegan's theory and adds dimension to the notion of an appropriate holding environment.

The question of developmental level was not asked in the design of PLS or in the research undertaken on its effects; however, such a question would be useful to ask in future research or replications of this program. My own study of a unique professional development vehicle in leadership training has sought to integrate the framework of adaptive leadership concepts and transformative learning—asking, essentially, did the learning of adaptive leadership lead to any kind of transformative learning? My assumption is that the value of PLS *cum* professional development, the positively meant description of it as "public therapy," and the collective value placed on it by its participants, lay with the sense that a kind of transformative learning had taken place—whether it was on the level of language (sociolinguistic) or attaining a new sense of self (psychological).

PLS as Transfer of Training

This study also analyzes findings through the transfer of training literature and, while not designed as a typical training program,[2] PLS nonetheless falls under a rubric that contains two frameworks from the transfer of training literature, both particularly apt for analyzing the data: the near/far transfer framework (Holton & Baldwin, 2003, pp. 7–8) and the "Work-Based Learning Pyramid" (Yorks, 2003, p. 143; Yorks, O'Neil, & Marsick, 1999, p. 14).

Table 5.3 Reported Changes: Near and Far Transfer of Learning

Superintendent	Reported Change/Effect of PLS	Example(s)	Near/Far
Maria	Increased empathy for adversaries	Coping with board members	Near
Maria	Recognition of role as lightning rod	Awareness of holding colleagues through the restructuring changes in her district	Far
Bobby	Increased ability to give work back to the group and not always be "the answer guy"	Allowing teachers to propose a school merger and allowing process to unfold	Near
Tom	Increased interest in using experiential learning for professional development of staff and teaching	Sent a principal to a highly experiential course to improve principal's performance, used Brian Malt's methods for teaching graduate students	Near
John	Increased awareness of the "dynamic tensions" in a system	Used metaphor of turning up the heat in the system to increase or decrease pressure "to move the system"	Far
Dee	Increased awareness of values others held	Partnered with representatives of African American community during a hiring decision for a new principal	Near
Dee	Increased curiosity about how perceived	Asked faculty consultant to conduct a 360-degree type of interviews with her peers so as to gain knowledge of how she was perceived	Far

Table 5.3 serves as an expansion of the initial summary of near and far transfer changes reported by the superintendents, by replicating that data from Table 5.1 and adding a third column to represent the dimension of near vs. far transfer of training.

As Table 5.3 suggests, the two female superintendents made greater leaps in their learning—i.e., "far transfers"—while just one of the three male superintendents had apparently done so. It would, however, be premature to conclude that women are more likely than men to engage in "high-road" (far) transfer. In this study's very small sample, the women in this cohort appear to have been highly regarded in their districts and thus may have been more inclined to make the more abstract, far-reaching leaps in applying their learning. The one male who, my judgment, also engaged in far transfer of learning (John) was able to do so only when he arrived in a less turbulent district than the one in which he served during PLS. Thus, stability of district may have been a factor in transfer distance.

The "work-based learning pyramid" was the second transfer of learning framework I found to be germane to the analysis of findings. While this pyramid was designed with the purpose of analyzing Action Learning and Communities of Practice as venues for learning (Yorks, 2003, p. 143), I see it as a useful construct for analyzing the program design of PLS. The pyramid is designed to represent four levels of learning goals.

Level One of the figure represents "problem-solving and implementation of solutions . . . opening up thinking around issues." Level Two represents the same level of learning as Level One, with the additional components of "problem reframing and problem setting; learning as a process for learning from work experience." Level Three comprises Level One and Level Two, in addition to which are "personal development goals and learning about learning styles." Level Four: The top level comprises Level One, Level Two, and Level Three, added to which are "personal and organizational transformation" (see Yorks, 2003, p. 143).

While PLS would have ideally set out to reach Level Four learning goals, the design of the program and the limited time and resources at its disposal did not allow for it to do so. Potential redesign of PLS might encompass personal learning goals and organizational transformation, as the teaching of adaptive leadership in a confrontational manner would often expose the weaknesses of someone's learning in unfamiliar psychological territory. In some cases, the superintendent-participant set out to learn more about herself (as in Dee's case), with the aid of a learning coach. In the final analysis of the sort of program PLS became for two years of a university executive education program, however, its overall content and achievements were largely located at Level Two. Problems were reframed, and the raw material of participants' district work lives was used as fodder for case presentations during the on-site sessions.

Summary

This chapter has explored the various dimensions of learning experienced by the PLS superintendents. Through a concise analysis of the data gleaned from my interviews, we have seen that the dimensions of race, external community dynamics, and personal traits in all likelihood affected the absorption and application of the concepts taught during PLS. At a more theoretical level, I have analyzed the linguistic elements of the program—an analysis that is largely speculative and suggestive of future research. At a more practice-oriented level, I have employed the literature of learning transfer of training. In this regard, the findings have been sifted anew and apart from the original research questions I set out to ask.

Notes

1. A reminder that the research questions that have informed this study are as follows:

    1. What concepts of PLS did participants learn, and how did they learn them?
    2. In what ways were superintendents able to apply concepts learned in PLS in the context of their jobs?
    3. In what ways (if any) was learning of PLS concepts similar to (or did it engender) transformative learning?

2. PLS was not a "typical training program" in the sense that its design was constantly shifting according to the needs of the superintendents. As a pilot program, its nature was fluid and experimental.

References

Blow, C. (2013, July 15). The whole system failed Trayvon Martin. *New York Times*. Retrieved from www.nytimes.com.

Burry, S. E. (2003). *Educational leadership theory and the phenomenon of the public school superintendent: A focus group study*. Doctoral dissertation. Retrieved from ProQuest Information and Learning Company (UMI No. 3080053).

Chace, S. (2017). What is 'the work' of breaking the zero-sum game? In A. Boitano, H. E. Schockman, and R. Lagomarsion (eds.), *Breaking the Zero-Sum Game: Transforming Society Through Inclusive Leadership* (pp. 195–208). Bingley: Emerald Group Publishing.

Collins, J. (2001). *Good to great*. New York, NY: HarperCollins Inc.

Cranton, P. A., & Roy, M. (2003). When the bottom falls out of the bucket: A holistic perspective on transformative learning. *Journal of Transformative Education*, 1(2), 86–98.

Drago-Severson, E. (2012). *Helping educators grow: Strategies and practices for leadership development*. Cambridge, MA: Harvard Education Press.

Eagleton, T. (1983). *Literary theory: An introduction*. Minneapolis, MN: University of Minnesota Press.

Elmore, R. F. (2000). *Building a new structure for school leadership*. Washington, DC: Albert Shanker Institute.

Erhard, W., Jensen, M. C., Zaffron, S., & Granger, K. L. (2012). *Creating leaders: An ontological/phenomenological model*. Working Paper. Harvard Business School Negotiations, Organizations and Markets Unit Research Paper Series No. 11-037; Barbados Group Working Paper No. 10-10; Simon School Working Paper No. FR-10-30. Retrieved from Social Sciences Research Network website: http://ssrn.com/abstract=1681682.

Freire, P. (1970). *Pedagogy of the oppressed*. New York, NY: Herder and Herder.

Glass, T. E., Bjork, L., & Brunner, C. C. (2000). *The study of the American school superintendency, 2000: A look at the superintendent of education in the new millennium*. Arlington, VA: American Association of School Administrators.

Greenleaf, R. K. (1977). *Servant leadership: A journey into the nature of legitimate power and greatness*. New York, NY: Paulist Press.

Grogan, M. (2000). Laying the groundwork for a reconception of the superintendency from feminist postmodern perspectives. *Educational Administration Quarterly*, 36(1), 117–142.

Guilleux, F. (2011). *A developmental perspective on leadership education of aspiring principals*. Doctoral dissertation. Retrieved from ProQuest Dissertations and Theses database (UMI No. 3471901).

Harris, R. (1990). *Language, Saussure, and Wittgenstein: How to play games with words*. London and New York, NY: Routledge.

Heifetz, R. (1994). *Leadership without easy answers*. Cambridge, MA: Harvard University Press.

Heifetz, R., Grashow, A., & Linsky, M. (2009). *The practice of adaptive leadership: Tools and tactics for changing your organization and the world*. Cambridge, MA: Harvard Business School Press.

Heifetz, R., & Linsky, M. (2004). When leadership spells danger. *Educational Leadership, 61*(7), 33–37.

Helsing, D., Howell, A., Kegan, R., & Lahey, L. L. (2008). Putting the "development" in professional development: Understanding and overturning educational leaders' immunities to change. *Harvard Educational Review, 78*(3), 437–465.

Hess, F. M. (1999). *Spinning wheels: The politics of urban school reform*. Washington, DC: Brookings Institution Press.

Hess, F. M. (2010). Weighing the case for school boards. *Phi Delta Kappan, 91*(6), 15–19.

Holton, E. F., & Baldwin, T. T. (2003). Making transfer happen: An action perspective on learning transfer systems. In E. F. Holton & T. T. Baldwin (Eds.), *Improving learning transfer in organizations*. San Francisco, CA: Jossey Bass.

Jentz, B. C., & Murphy, J. T. (2005). Embracing confusion: What leaders do when they don't know what to do. *Phi Delta Kappan, 86*(5), 358–366.

Kuhn, T. S. (1970). *The structure of scientific revolutions*. Chicago, IL: University of Chicago Press.

Labov, W. (1972). *Language in the inner city: Studies in the Black English vernacular*. Philadelphia, PA: University of Pennsylvania Press.

Levine, A. (2005). *Educating school leaders*. Washington, DC: Education Schools Project.

Meyerson, D.E. (2001). *Tempered radicals: How people use difference to inspire change at work*. Boston, MA: Harvard Business School Press.

Montero, M. (2011). Problematization. Wiley Online Library. Retrieved from https://doi.org/10.1002/9780470672532.wbepp220.

Murphy, J., Moorman, H. N., & McCarthy, M. (2008). A framework for rebuilding initial certification and preparation programs in educational leadership: Lessons from whole state reform initiatives. *Teachers College Record, 110*, 2172–2203.

National Center for Education and the Economy. (2007). *Tough choices or tough times*. Retrieved from http://www.ncee.org/wp-content/uploads/2010/04/Executive-Summary.pdf.

Ortiz, F.I. & Ortiz, D.J. (1995). How gender and ethnicity interact in the practice of educational administration: The case of Hispanic female superintendents. In R. Donmoyer, M. –Imber & J. J. Scheurich (Eds.), *The knowledge base in educational administration: Multiple perspectives* (pp. 158–173). Albany, NY: State University of New York Press.

Parks, S. D. (2005). *Leadership can be taught: A bold approach for a complex world*. Cambridge, MA: Harvard Business School Press.

Pedler, M. (1991). Questioning ourselves. In M. Pedler (Ed.), *Action leaning in practice* (2nd ed., pp. 63070). Brookfield, VT: Gower. Revans, R.W. (1982). *The origin and growth of action learning*. London: Chartwell Bratt.

Revans, R.W. (1989). *The golden jubilee of action learning*. Manchester, England: Manchester Action Learning Exchange, University of Manchester.

Salomon, G., & Perkins, D.N. (1989). Rocky roads to transfer: Rethinking mechanisms of a neglected phenomenon. *Educational Psychologist, 24*, 113–142.

Teitel, L. (2005). Supporting school system leaders. (Working Papers, Center for Public Leadership). Cambridge, MA: Harvard University Press

Teitel, L. (2006). *Supporting school system leaders: The state of effective training programs for school superintendents*. New York, NY: Wallace Foundation.

Yorks, L. (2003). Beyond the classroom: Transfer from work-based learning initiatives. In E. F. Holton & T. T. Baldwin (Eds.), *Improving learning transfer in organizations*. San Francisco, CA: Jossey-Bass.

Yorks, L., O'Neil, J., & Marsick, V. J. (Eds.) (1999a). *Action learning: Successful strategies for individual, team, and organizational development*. San Francisco, CA: Berrett-Koehler.

6 Conclusions and Recommendations for Future Research

This qualitative case study sought to explore the learning of a handful of superintendents of complex urban districts engaged in a unique Action Learning program tailored to their needs. They participated in a two-year executive training program based on the principles of adaptive leadership developed by Heifetz and Sinder (1991a, 1991b), and Williams (2005). This program is defined as an Action Learning program because superintendents co-created the curriculum during the sessions as they brought their various cases for discussion and analysis to both the large-group setting of the program and to the smaller breakout groups. During the PLS training, it was clear that the superintendents benefited from their learning and enjoyed the program. The abiding question that remained following the program's termination was whether or not the learning they experienced had stayed with the participants—and if so, in what ways had they applied it. On a deeper level, the study asked if participants underwent transformative learning as a result of their engagement with and participation in PLS. By employing methods of qualitative inquiry, through interviews with PLS participants, their colleagues, and document analysis, I found that the learning for the vast majority of the PLS cohort remained and adhered, and in some cases affected them not only on their jobs but on deeper levels of their being.

Summary of Findings

What I discovered in undertaking this study was as follows:

1. The cohort adopted three diagnostic tools of adaptive leadership to assist them in their jobs: the concepts of 1) Managing Disequilibrium and 2) Diagnosing Stakeholder Values were universally referred to in their interviews and assisted superintendents in meeting the challenges of their districts. 3) In addition, the adaptation of the terms Technical Work and Adaptive Work were referred to. This finding relates to my first research question (RQ1): What concepts of PLS did participants learn, and how did they learn them?

Conclusions and Recommendations 115

2. For the majority of the cohort the contexts in which they operated comprised two main challenges: those of their school boards and those presented by the politics of their communities. This finding connects to my second research question (RQ2): In what ways were superintendents able to apply concepts learned in PLS in the context of their jobs?
3. The third major finding for this study also pertains to RQ2: For the majority of the superintendents, the application of adaptive leadership concepts learned during PLS had a positive effect on the perceptions they held of their situations.
4. The fourth major finding for this study relates to transformative learning. The majority of superintendents reported their learning in a way that suggested having undergone some sort of learning akin to transformative learning in the sociolinguistic domain. This finding answers the question posed in my third research question (RQ3): In what ways (if any) was learning of PLS concepts similar to (or did it engender) transformative learning?
5. The fifth major finding relates to the context of superintendents' training and preparation. Of the superintendents interviewed and discussed here, all testified to PLS as a highly valuable form of professional development. This finding relates most directly to RQ2.

Research Question 1: What Concepts of PLS Did Participants Learn, and How Did They Learn Them?

Nine concepts of adaptive leadership formed the pillars of learning for PLS:

1. Diagnosing Stakeholder Value
2. Managing Disequilibrium
3. Technical vs. Adaptive Work
4. Distribution of Loss at a Rate the Group Can Tolerate
5. Getting to the Balcony and Seeing the Dance Floor
6. Staying Alive
7. Orchestrating Conflict
8. Listening for the Song Beneath the Words
9. Distinguishing between Formal and Informal Authority

Of these concepts, the majority of the participating superintendents resonated with the first four and most especially with the first two. Given the nature of the urban school superintendent's job—what has been called "an impossible job" (Fuller et al., 2003) and "the toughest job in America" (PBS, 2000)—it is not surprising that diagnostic tools such as Diagnosing Stakeholder Values and Managing Disequilibrium would be absorbed and utilized by superintendents. The fact that their jobs are riddled with confusion (Jentz & Murphy, 2005) would explain the appeal of diagnosis, as well as their use of the terms technical work vs. adaptive work as a way to see their way through this confusion. The constant challenges of politics, board turnover, and an ever-increasing set of mandates, explain why any superintendent would want to manage disequilibrium. Discovering language for this general situation of problematic reality was a powerful experience for the superintendents, and the power of their learning was reflected in their interviews with me. (It should be remembered that I did my best not to "lead the witness" in my questions and allowed the superintendents to describe their learning in their own way and in their own time during interviews.) The number of times that the top two concepts of PLS emerged in the interviews with superintendents emerged organically.

The first part of this research question, "What concepts of PLS did participants learn," was answered directly. The second part of the question was answered less precisely; the "how" of the superintendents' learning was hidden from view, although indirect evidence emerged indicating that superintendents had experimented with the concepts both during and following the sessions of PLS. The "how" of learning forms a complex question worthy of further study and is explored briefly in "Recommendations for Further Research."

Research Question 2: In What Ways Were Superintendents Able to Apply Concepts Learned in PLS in the Context of Their Jobs?

This research question is answered by the main finding that, as a result of their engagement with PLS, both during and after, superintendents began to see a shift in the gestalt of their jobs in a positive way. This discovery in some cases led to more positive interactions with their boards and communities. It certainly seemed to lead to a more positive conceptualization of themselves. In some cases, such as Bobby's, the superintendent no longer felt that he had to have all the answers immediately. This new view of himself led Bobby to engage in an issue over creating a new school in a new way, where he was able to "give the work back to the group"—in other words, to not take on the responsibility for providing "all the answers" (in Bobby's words, defaulting to being "the answer guy") for the district's dilemmas himself, but rather probing the group he worked with for answers. Bobby likely learned this from the style of case-in-point teaching employed during PLS, where the pedagogical model was that of putting questions back on the group, in lieu of providing bromides about leadership. Throughout the cohort, there was a sense that a new gestalt of the job of urban school superintendent as a political actor was possible, as was a more practical way of looking at what John called the "dynamic tensions" of their environments.

Research Question 3: In What Ways (If Any) Was Learning of PLS Concepts Similar to (or Did it Engender) Transformative Learning?

Recent literature (e.g. Helsing, Howell, Kegan, & Lahey, 2008; Erhard, Jensen, Zaffron, & Granger 2012), suggests that adaptive leadership and transformative learning may share similar intentions for those who undertake adult learning. Where Heifetz discusses "blind spots" illuminated through the diagnostic tools of adaptive leadership, Mezirow points to a discarding of assumptions that are no longer workable. What both theorists refer to is the notion of adult development occurring as a result of a widening lens upon oneself or one's situation. Thus, a blind spot for a person endeavoring to exercise leadership might be her habit of discounting the voices of people of color in a given dialogue. An assumption discarded could be that of a lifestyle choice (e.g., a "social drinking" habit assumed to be under control is, through the process of a disorienting dilemma, recognized as problematic and harmful). Transformative learning, however, is a more nuanced theory and has been more widely and deeply discussed in the literature of adult learning, while adaptive leadership is in a more inchoate phase of theoretical development. The number of studies that use transformative learning as a conceptual lens outnumbers the number of studies that use adaptive leadership in this way, although the latter number is increasing.

The overall question I explored in this study revolved around the learning experienced by a certain idiosyncratic group of learners in a particular professional situation. The primary research question concerned which of the PLS adaptive leadership concepts were learned, and which remained with the superintendents following the learning sessions. The secondary research question then asked how the superintendents applied their learning in context. Once this learning was ascertained, the next question asked the depth to which the learning had penetrated. This question seemed best articulated and viewed via the lens of transformative learning.

When asking if transformative learning took place, I extracted two constructs proposed by Mezirow: 1) that of the six main habits of mind through which an adult learner might experience a shift in perspective: epistemic, sociolinguistic, psychological, philosophical, moral-ethical, and aesthetic, and 2) that of the construct of the 10 steps of transformative learning, beginning with a "disorienting dilemma" and ending with "a reintegration into one's life on the basis of conditions dictated by one's new perspectives" (Mezirow, 2000, p. 22).

Sifting the data through the lens of these two constructs, I found that although the superintendents all experienced some elements of transformative learning, the most densely clustered transformative learning occurred in the realm of shifts in habits of mind—implicitly held biases or paradigms—particularly in the realm of sociolinguistic habits of mind. Future research studies might consider positioning these questions aimed at extracting data where they will show whether and how participants might have experienced the 10 steps of transformative learning in an experiential Action Learning program such as PLS, and future studies.

Summary

This qualitative research study has yielded a number of findings about the lived experiences of urban school superintendents as they absorbed and applied concepts taught in an executive education leadership training program, one whose curriculum was largely based on the diagnostic tools comprising adaptive leadership. The questions this study has asked may be paraphrased thus: *What did superintendents learn, how did they apply their learning, and was their learning in any way transformative?* The answers to these research questions have been explored in-depth and are in some cases unexpected. As we have seen, the main concepts learned in PLS concerned managing turbulence in their districts, and this management seemed to be enhanced by embracing the notion of diagnosing stakeholders' values. The cohort developed a universal appreciation for terms that articulated their challenges such as "adaptive work" versus "technical work"—i.e., the parsing of the difference between those challenges whose sources and solutions seemed clear, and those whose sources and solutions appeared to be less clear. Through the lens of transformative learning, most superintendents seemed to have experienced learning that was akin to transformative learning in the sociolinguistic domain. As cited in Chapter 4 (FN3), "Sociolinguistic perspectives are the way we view social norms, culture, and *how we use language* [emphasis added]" (Cranton & Roy, 2003, p. 88). However, the contexts in which the superintendents worked also emerged as critical factors as superintendents attempted to apply their learning on the job. In many cases a new gestalt emerged for the superintendents, as they began to form new images of how they could do their work and "stay alive" in the process—i.e., to keep their jobs, maintain their political capital, and/or eschew becoming marginalized.

The old saw "when it's the individual against the system, the system wins" is vividly illustrated in the picture of a well-intentioned superintendent struggling to get things done within a web of political forces. The overall conclusion that emerges from the stories and testimonies of these superintendents is that the "entire system of influences" (Holton & Baldwin, 2003, p. 6) plays into the equation of whether and if an investment in leadership training will pay off. In terms of transfer of learning, this "system of influences" is made up of the climate in which the learner wishes to transfer his or her learning, the "personal characteristics" (or developmental level) of the participants, and the program design (Holton & Baldwin, 2003, p. 6). Given the overall climate in urban districts currently, I have come to the following four conclusions about the effects of PLS:

1. Adaptive leadership concepts provide a way out of the confusion for superintendents by giving them language by which to articulate their dilemmas. Having attained the language, the superintendents were now better able, in many cases, to address these dilemmas more forcefully. Throughout the cohort, from the most enthusiastic participants to the least, language was adopted and assimilated into superintendents' thinking.
2. The key variable in application of superintendents' learning was that of district climate. When superintendents were in positions of relative stability in terms of their own job security, even during turbulent times they were inclined to experiment with using adaptive leadership concepts in working with their staff or approaching their jobs. Maria's case of shepherding her colleagues through a seismic district restructuring exemplifies a superintendent in such a scenario. Dee's case exemplifies another scenario of superintendent stability, where both her position and her district's structure appeared to be relatively stable. She was able to be successfully proactive in a politically fraught situation.
3. The implications of sociolinguistic transformative learning for the superintendents appeared to have been linked to critical reflection, or "getting on the balcony." Again, the introduction of new language played a key role in expanding the horizons of the PLS participants. As Yorks (2003), invoking Mezirow, puts it, "Critical reflection [is] a process through which people recognize that their perceptions are filtered through uncritically accepted views, beliefs, attitudes, and feelings. . . . This kind of reflection fosters what Argyris and Schön (1978) have termed double-loop learning" (p. 147). Double-loop learning is a metaphor used for more complex types of learning than input-output. It is a way of suggesting more a nuanced view of a situation, where more questions are asked than are answered. To engage in double-loop learning is to elevate a perspective beyond a known problem and a known solution. It is another way of articulating adaptive work. Thus, the very act of "getting on the balcony" is an act of adaptive leadership.
4. Some degree of learning transfer occurred for the PLS superintendents. While this was not one of the research questions, transfer of learning—which might be defined, broadly, as occurring "when one effectively acts on [an] altered interpretation" of a given situation (Yorks, 2003, p. 151)—indeed took place for most of the PLS superintendents at least some of the time.

Recommendations

In this section, I offer a series of recommendations for leadership training programs and for research, based upon my experiences of both managing and conducting research on PLS.

Recommendations for the Field of Adaptive Leadership

Adaptive leadership is a widely recognized construct in the field of leadership studies and in the world of management consulting. Numerous articles have appeared about adaptive leadership in publications such as the *Harvard Business Review*. Increasingly, dissertation studies use adaptive leadership as a conceptual lens, and more and more journal articles are emerging that explore adaptive leadership in combination with other systemic theories, such as complexity theory (cf. Uhl-Bien, Marion, & McKelvey, 2007). To my knowledge, however, no executive education training programs based on adaptive leadership have extended beyond a few weeks—with the exception of PLS. In addition, little empirical evidence has appeared as to the efficacy of such trainings. Guilleux's 2010 study of a five-day experiential leadership education course for school principals and O'Brien's 2016 study of case-in-point learning in graduate courses at Harvard stand as an exception, but they are at the vanguard (Guilleux, 2011; O'Brien, 2016).

Theoretically, adaptive leadership is part of an intellectual lineage that can be traced back to Freud. The literature on group dynamics that speaks to notions of parallel process could enhance the design of a new study on adaptive leadership teaching and its effects. If, for example, one were to replicate a program such as PLS, it would be interesting to consider where the adaptive challenge lies at the state level as well as at the district level. Research questions could be designed to inquire whether district challenges reflect state challenges and whether these challenges manifest in any of the schools. Which sorts of leadership intervention tactics would work at the state or district levels? How do the challenges the superintendent encounters on the board reflect the larger community? What sort of measures could be used to gauge the "ripeness" of the community for a leadership intervention?

The superintendents, as has been stated repeatedly throughout this narrative, were profoundly challenged by the politics both within and outside of their boards. If, in the teaching and learning of adaptive leadership, we were to focus on the tendency of groups in the midst of an adaptive challenge to look for technical solutions and help them determine what kind of a challenge it was that they were facing, a fundamental change might be brought about in the understanding of a superintendent's choices within a highly politicized urban district.

Recommendations for the Training of School Administrators

I have explored many aspects of superintendent learning in PLS; I did not, however, formulate research questions about the value of the network that the program provided for superintendents. Nor did I formulate questions about the value of the faculty consultants. Nonetheless, these aspects of the program emerged as invaluable to the group and cannot be overemphasized in the program's training. In Orr's 2006 study of superintendent preparation, the need for a "safe space" as a holding environment for their learning "was underscored" by participants in her study (Orr, 2006, p. 1393)—a need consistent with my own observations of PLS while in session, and during my interviews with participants. Throughout the PLS sessions, the sense of trust the superintendents placed in one another was palpable.

A high level of trust was also placed in certain of the faculty consultant coaches assigned to the participants. All of the superintendents were offered a faculty consultant and about half of the participants mentioned their relationships with their assigned consultant in a positive light: Tom, Dee, and John. Of the three who mentioned their consultant in their interviews, Dee reported that she had retained her consultant beyond the termination of the program. Tom also spoke specifically about the value of the "coaching" element of the program.

> I think to just go to [PLS sessions] and not [have] had the follow-up [with the faculty consultants] would have been a loss. There's a lot more continuity to it. It means that you don't forget the relationship and you can't pretend it didn't happen. It also gives you a chance to practice and internalize what you're learning . . . So I thought that was an important part of the process.

In a future redesign of PLS, I would recommend the use of such coaches, with a study that isolates them as a variable in outcomes of learning.

Although Foundation R. chose not to extend PLS in its original form, its reputation as a program of high value to superintendents—not least because of the value of forming communities of practice as "safe spaces"—began to spread. Following the termination of PLS in 2004, a state commissioner of education invited two of its lead faculty instructors to duplicate the adaptive leadership training they had taught in the program in a modified form for superintendents throughout his Northeastern state. Out of these trainings, a series of "round tables" was formed, where superintendents who had undergone this training met on a monthly basis to discuss their leadership challenge cases. On a few such occasions, I was invited to facilitate these discussions—serving essentially in the role of a faculty consultant for an abbreviated replication of PLS and supporting the holding environment of this network. The value of the diagnostic terms that commonly stem from the construct of adaptive leadership was again felt by superintendents in the field to provide what Guilleux terms "linguistic support" (Guilleux, 2011, p. iv) for their dilemmas. Future iterations of training programs modeled on PLS might do well to study the value-add of coaches between learning sessions and emphasize the creation of a high-trust holding environment.

Finally, I would recommend adaptive leadership as a training methodology for superintendents because it addresses the need for a more tightly intertwined relationship between theory and practice. The theory of adaptive leadership is based on the discovery of effective practice, and Murphy et al.'s image of a strand of DNA is useful in the application of this theory—as theory and practice intertwine.

Recommendations for the Theory of Transformative Learning

Mezirow and others have provided articulations for the learning adults experience when their assumptions have become unsettled. Transformative learning occurs when assumptions—which form the basis for perspectives or habits of mind—begin to shift. Through the shedding, expansion, and reconfiguring of assumptions, such reasoning asserts, adults may become more authentically themselves. These ideas provide a more robust theoretical grounding for adaptive leadership and the intersection of these two constructs (i.e., adaptive leadership and transformative learning) has been noted.

A third construct for meaning-making in adult learning is Kegan's constructivist-developmental theory of "orders of mind," which he has articulated as "not just the way [an adult] behaves, not just the way he feels, but the way he knows—not just what he knows but the way he knows" (Kegan, 1994, p. 17). Kegan has developed the notion of "orders of mind" in terms of subjectivity and objectivity, and his five orders of mind provide a theoretical scaffold. Perspective shift, or transformation in habits of mind—what Kegan calls an order of mind—is a place of nexus for studying how adults develop.

The idea of a blended definition for transformative learning is not altogether new: As Drago-Severson (2009) has written (citing Kegan, Mezirow, and others),

> With transformative learning . . . a qualitative shift occurs in *how a person actively interprets, organizes, understands, and makes sense of his or her experience* [emphasis in original]. This kind of learning is associated with an increase in individual developmental capacities, which enables a person to have a broader perspective on him- or herself, on others, and on the relationship between self and others.
>
> (p. 11)

Here I would recommend measuring these capacities through Kegan's Subject-Object Interview (SOI), as O'Brien has done in his research (cf., O'Brien, 2016), to assess complexity of mind (Guilleux, 2011, pp. 64–65).[1] Findings from the SOI might then be used to design the next iteration of benchmarking habits of mind, which might take the form of creating an interview that would assess orientation in the six domains of habits of mind: epistemic, sociolinguistic, psychological, moral-ethical, philosophical, and aesthetic (Cranton & Roy, 2003, p. 88). Following the "intervention" (such as a PLS program) the interviews might be administered again. Any shift in orientation would provide findings for analysis, and perhaps generate new research on the intersectionality of constructive-developmental theory and transformative learning. An interesting dimension to add to such a study design would be to assess the strength of a holding environment for such a program as PLS.

Recommendations for Research

As adaptive leadership is in its infancy, I suggest the expansion and development of studies such as the one undertaken here. In addition to employing Kegan's SOI, an interview instrument designed to measure the capacity for leading adaptively might be developed. A similar such instrument might be developed to measure whether and how transformative learning had occurred—asking, for example, what assumptions were held prior to participating in a leadership development program and in its wake. A researcher might also create research questions that seek to gather data on whether transformative learning was epochal or incremental (see Priestley's 2009 study on the initial rejection and eventual acceptance of "homosexuality" by "heterosexuals"). In terms of professional development, the key definition of transfer of training concerns "the application of knowledge, skills and attitudes" (Cheng & Ho, 2001, p. 103). These three dimensions could be connected to transformative learning and a propensity for adaptive leadership. For example, the "knowledge" dimension could be measured in terms of self-knowledge, the "skills" dimension in terms of political astuteness and success (for example, longevity in a district), and the "attitude" dimension might be measured via a questionnaire about assumptions. Yet these dimensions fail to account for the protean nature of urban districts. Thus, the fundamental research question remains: How can one measure the stability of a political environment? Here I would suggest looking at board elections and demographic data—such as poverty index—and the recent rate of turnover in superintendents.

The optimal way to ascertain the effectiveness of a program such as PLS would contain quantitative elements. For example, would longevity in a district be a mark of success? Other marks of success might include steady (as opposed to dramatically spiked) increases in student test scores or reductions in teacher turnover. Additional benchmarks might also be established along the lines of a longitudinal study. For example, interviews could be conducted prior to participation, immediately following completion of the program, six months following, and a year following.

Another means to generate and interpret data would be the conducting of interviews, using a greater number of peers and coworkers and such measures as a "360-degree feedback." This popular self-assessment tool asks for employees to distribute questionnaires about their own behavior to people who work above them, below them, and at their own level and to provide honest anonymous feedback. The image of "360" refers to the image of a circle, with the idea being that persons at different levels of an organization could provide a full circle's worth—all possible, 360 degrees—of perspectives on a given person requiring such feedback. To extend the metaphor, the person to whom the feedback is then given resides at the center of the circle. These sorts of interviews could also be conducted before and after the program and followed up incrementally over a number of years. Such forms of qualitative research would ground the study in important ways, offering more reliable data with a broader and complex "observing" population.

The critical elements of PLS's pedagogy that fell outside the scope of this study lay with the fact that the grant from Foundation R. allowed for faculty consultants to travel to superintendents' districts to reinforce the teaching that had occurred in session. While briefly touched upon in this chapter, this aspect of the program design was highly beneficial when it worked.

In sum, before seeking to replicate a program such as PLS for the purposes of research, great care should be taken in designing pre-program measures, and ascertaining whether and how progress, in fact, has been made.

Reflections

This study is the outcome of a long and rich relationship with education. I began my career as a teacher in the early 1990s at a private school for girls, similar to the one I had attended as a child. By the mid-90s, I was no longer satisfied with teaching such an elite set of students and was drawn to the charter school movement; in 1996, I became a founding teacher of a small urban charter school in Massachusetts. It was during this time that the issue of "leadership" and systemic dysfunctions made themselves felt to me and my colleagues as our daily work was buffeted by political turmoil surrounding the creation of charter schools. By the time I left, faculty turnover was estimated at 70% annually.

It was for these reasons that I was drawn to a policy school for a mid-career master's in public administration, where I encountered experiential pedagogical methods and became an avid student of adaptive leadership. The diagnostic tools of adaptive leadership gave me a language to express what I had experienced during four turbulent years of teaching in the politically charged atmosphere of a charter school. When I was invited to assist in the creation and implementation of a leadership training program for urban school superintendents, it was my hope that my aspirations to better the environment in which children are given access to free education would be realized. I was fascinated to witness the alacrity with which the PLS participants took hold of the adaptive leadership concepts.

This narrative is an attempt to capture, within the frame of qualitative research and retrospective recall, some of the richness of learning that occurred during those two years of PLS's existence, from May 2002 through May 2004. I consider it a privilege to have been involved in the conception of this program, and thus to have witnessed the growth of this unique group of education professionals. Within each of their stories resides a piece of the larger story of public education in America. Their challenges reflect the systemic challenges of our society with regard to education.

Another aspect of the program not fully explored in the research, and one not fully articulated as the program unfolded, was that of parallel process, discussed earlier in this chapter. A certain amount of chaos pervaded the program as superintendent participants came and went, due to turn over in their districts. Fully half of the participating superintendents were either fired, took jobs in another district, or left the professional altogether within the two years of PLS's duration. There was also turnover in the underwriting foundation's staff, which in turn affected the duration of PLS. During the focus group interview, superintendents spoke of "lobbying" with the foundation to continue PLS in its present form, but that was not to be. Instead, another executive program took its place at the university where PLS was housed—one that had its own brand of excellence, but which was not as squarely situated in the teaching and learning of adaptive leadership. The "churning" nature of these changes reflected the system we endeavored to effect.

The notion of a holding environment, while not original to adaptive leadership, in many ways forms the core of its pedagogy. The container in which the work of learning could take place was made stronger by the trust the PLS participants had in one another and in those responsible for the teaching and execution of the program. If society's container for education were made stronger—by, for example, according teachers and educators the respect they enjoy in other countries, such as Finland—there might be greater hope for the future of education and for the well-being of this country.

Note

1. The SOI is structured as follows: "The ninety-minute interview involves the participants telling stories parked by six key words (Angry, Success, Strong Stand or Conviction, Important to Me, Torn, and Change)" (Guilleux, 2011, pp. 64–65).

References

Argyris, C., & Schön, D. (1978). *Organizational learning: A theory of action perspective*. Reading, MA: Addison-Wesley.

Cheng, W. L., & Ho, C. K. (2001). A review of transfer of training studies in the past decade. *Personnel Review, 30*(1), 102–118. doi:10.1108/00483480110380163

Cranton, P. A., & Roy, M. (2003). When the bottom falls out of the bucket: A holistic perspective on transformative learning. *Journal of Transformative Education, 1*(2), 86–98.

Drago-Severson, E. (2009). *Leading adult learning: Supporting adult development in our schools*. Thousand Oaks, CA: Corwin Press.

Erhard, W., Jensen, M. C., Zaffron, S., & Granger, K. L. (2012). *Creating leaders: An ontological/phenomenological model*. Working Paper. Harvard Business School Negotiations, Organizations and Markets Unit Research Paper Series No. 11-037; Barbados Group Working Paper No. 10-10; Simon School Working Paper No. FR-10-30. Retrieved from Social Sciences Research Network website: http://ssrn.com/abstract=1681682

Fuller, H., Campbell, C., Celio, M. B., Harvey, J., Immerwahr, J., & Winger, A. (2003). *An impossible job: The view from the urban superintendent's chair*. Seattle, WA: Center on Reinventing Public Education.

Guilleux, F. (2011). *A developmental perspective on leadership education of aspiring principals*. Doctoral dissertation. Retrieved from ProQuest Dissertations and Theses database (UMI No. 3471901).

Heifetz, R., & Sinder, R. (1991a). Teaching and assessing leadership courses: Part one. *National Forum, 71*(1), 21. Retrieved from Academic Search Premier database.

Heifetz, R., & Sinder, R. (1991b). Teaching and assessing leadership courses: Part two. *National Forum, 71*(2), 36. Retrieved from Academic Search Premier database.

Helsing, D., Howell, A., Kegan, R., & Lahey, L. L. (2008). Putting the "development" in professional development: Understanding and overturning educational leaders' immunities to change. *Harvard Educational Review, 78*(3), 437–465.

Holton, E. F., & Baldwin, T. T. (2003). Making transfer happen: An action perspective on learning transfer systems. In E. F. Holton & T. T. Baldwin (Eds.), *Improving learning transfer in organizations*. San Francisco, CA: Jossey Bass.

Jentz, B. C., & Murphy, J. T. (2005). Embracing confusion: What leaders do when they don't know what to do. *Phi Delta Kappan, 86*(5), 358–366.

Kegan, R. (1982). *The evolving self: Problem and process in human development*. Cambridge, MA: Harvard University Press.

Kegan, R. (1994). *In over our heads: The mental demands of modern life*. Cambridge, MA: Harvard University Press.

Merrow, J. (Writer). (2000, September). *Toughest job in America*. PBS. The Merrow Report. Arlington, VA: Public Broadcasting Station.

Mezirow, J. (2000). Learning to think like and adult: Core concepts of transformation theory. In J. Mezirow & Associates (Eds.), *Learning as transformation:*

Critical perspectives on a theory in progress (pp. 3–33). San Francisco, CA: Jossey Bass.

O'Brien, T. J. (2016). *Looking for development in leadership development: Impacts of experiential and constructivist methods on graduate students and graduate schools.* Doctoral dissertation. Retrieved from: https://dash.harvard.edu/bitstream/handle/1/27112706/OBRIEN-DISSERTATION-2016.pdf?sequence=1&isAllowed=y

Orr, M. T. (2006). Learning the superintendency: Socialization, negotiation, and determination. *Teachers College Record, 108*(7), 1362–1403. doi:10.1111/j.1467-9620.2006.00697.x

Priestley, T. L. (2009). *Learning to unlearn: A case study of the initial rejection and subsequent acceptance of homosexuality by heterosexuals.* Doctoral dissertation. Retrieved from ProQuest Dissertations and Theses database (UMI No. 3368425).

Uhl-Bien, M., Marion, R., & McKelvey, B. (2007). Complexity leadership theory: Shifting leadership from the industrial age to the knowledge era. *Leadership Quarterly, 18*(4), 298–318.

Williams, D. (2005). *Real leadership.* San Francisco, CA: Berett-Kohler.

Yorks, L. (2003). Beyond the classroom: Transfer from work-based learning initiatives. In E. F. Holton & T. T. Baldwin (Eds.), *Improving learning transfer in organizations.* San Francisco, CA: Jossey Bass.

Index

achievement gap 50, 69–70
ACLU 17
action learning 110, 114, 118
adaptive challenge 5, 6, *41*, 71, 80, 99, 102, 106, 120
adaptive change 42, 59, 64, 69, 74, 106
adaptive work 56
adult learning 3, 80, 90, 117, 122
ally 52–53
Argyris, C. 65, 119
artifacts 38, 47, 90
aspirations *vs*. realities 33
authority 4, 8, 31, 39, 41, *41*, 43, 61, 68, 115; formal *vs*. informal 8, 68, 73-74, 115

balcony, being on the 6, 25, 51, 54, 67, 87, 91, 106, 115, 119
benchmark 72, 123–124
Bennis, Warren 4
blind spots 27, 38, 117
Bloomberg, Michael 2
boards *see* school board
bridge metaphor 90
budget 44, 54

case-in-point learning 30, 33, 120
case-in-point teaching 31, 32, 78, 85, 90–91, 108, 116
case presentation 85–86
change (as loss) 25, 56
change (structural, systemic) 25, 50
class 17, 68, 69, 72
coaching 121–122
collapse of sense-making 34
community 26, 51, 54, 87, 101
conceptual vitamins 33
confidante 52–53

confidentiality 37
configuration *see* gestalt
conflict 7, 21, 22, 24, 57, 78
constraints of authority 39
consultants (PLS) 19, 36, 43–44, 54, 76, 83–86, **82**, **92**, 104, **109**, 121, 124
contexts 25, 47, 51, **54**, 100, 115
critical thinking 77

dangerous leadership 53, 67
diagnosing stakeholder values 5, 41, 42, 91, 115
disequilibrium 5, 45, 52, 105
disequilibrium, management of *see* managing disequilibrium
disoriented 43
disorienting dilemma 72, 78, 80, 117
distributing loss 6, 64–67, 106, 115
double-loop learning 119

Elmore, Richard 48–49, 55, 101
empathy 24, 48, 56, 58, 63, 73, 75, 78, 87, **92**, 95, **95**, 98–100, **109**
espoused theory 65
ethnicity **13**, 17, 21, 54, 101
experiential learning 2
external mandates 25–26, **25**, 47, 50, 54

factions 4, 5, 15, 18, 20, 24, 42, 48, 56, 57–58, 66–67, 74, 96–97, 101
formal authority *see* authority
fractals 8, 32
Frost, Robert 39

gestalt 25, 51–55, **51**, 67, 80, 103–104, 116, 118
group dynamics 4, 21, 31–32, 49
group facilitation 31

Hall, Beverly 2
heat 2, 5–6, 15–16, 59, 60, 74, 92–93, 97–99, **103**
Heifetz, Ronald 1, 2, 4, 5, 7, 22, 32, 39, 52, 53, 59, 63, 64, 67, 74, 75, 80, 87, 92, 99, 100, 105–106, 114, 117
"here and now" teaching *see* case-in-point teaching
Hess, Frederick 93–94, 96, 102
hidden issue 26, 27, 30
holding environment 29, 31, 45, 55, 107–108, 121–122, 123

informal authority *see* authority
informational learning 80
initial event 32, 33, 37
instructional core 25, 26, 47–49, 54
integrating new perspectives 72. 78, 79
intervention 4

Keith, Kent 39
Kennedy, Robert xii
King, Martin Luther, Jr. xii
Klein, Joel 2

language 21, 33, 55, 64, 73–75, 86, 87, 91, 93, 99, 100, 103, 105–106, 108, 116, 119
learning transfer *see* transfer of learning
lightning rod 15, 16
linguistic revolution 105
linguistic theory 3, 4, 100, 105
listening, for the song 7, 39, 68
literary theory 105
loss, distribution of 6, 64–67
lottery system 24
low-road transfer 80, 93

managing disequilibrium 5, 15, 20, 41, 42, 59–63, 65, 77, 87, 93–95, 97–100, 106, 114, 115, 118
Martin, Trayvon 96
mayoral control 102
Mezirow, Jack 72, 90–91, 105, 108, 117, 119, 122
money 26, 27
music exercise 7, 39, 40
music of conflict 7

National Association for the Advancement of Colored People (NAACP) 17, 20, 57, 62, 98
network 83, **83**, 86, 121–122
No Child Left Behind (NCLB) xii, 2, 40, 50, 69
Not in My Backyard (NIMBY) 17, 57

orchestrating conflict 7, 68, 97, 115
orders of mind 122
organizational behavior 33
Orwell, George 38

paradigm shift 104
parallel process 30–32, 100, 120, 125
partnering 20
people skills 102
pizza diagram 5, 42, 57–58, 67, 71, 74, 106
politics 25, 26, 30, 49, 55–56, 61, 63, 66, 87, 91, 94, 96, 100–101, 104, 114, 115, 116, 118, 120, 123
problematic realities 100
professional development 80–81, 84
public therapy (PLS as) 42–43, 78, 80, 83, 108

Q learning 103
qualitative methodology 34–36

race 14, 49, 54, 56, 58, 61, 68, 69–70, 72, 76, 95–96, 110
Rhee, Michelle 63, 65–69, 71–72
role-playing exercise (simulation) 83, 84, 86
Rost, Joseph 4

safe space 107, 121
salary 26, 27
school board 15, 25, 26, 42, 48, 51, 53–56, 60–61, 67, 71–72, 87, 91, 92, 100–102, 114–116, 120, 123
schools: of choice 18, 25, 49, 60, 65–66, 74; public 16, 17, 25–26, 62, 66, 68, 72
self-awareness 27
sense-making 34
servant leadership 98
shifts in perspective 72–77, 80, 93, 105, 117, 122
small group work 44
Snowden, D. 8

sociolinguistic learning 72–75, 73, 80, 87, 105, 108, 115, 117–119, 123
soft power 8
stakeholder values 5, 17, 24, 41–42, 53, 55–59, 60, 62, 63, 71, 74, 87, 91, 93–100, 106, 114
standardized tests 2, 6, 31, 50
staying Alive 7, 67–68, 115, 118
stew 5, 15, 57, 59, 60, 87
structural/systemic change 25, 25, 26, 47, 50, 54
subject object interview (SOI) 123, 126
superintendents *see* urban school superintendent

technical work 6, 44, 64, 70, 71, 80, 87, 91, 93, 99, 102, 105–106, 114–116, 118
tempered radicals 98–99
theory-in-use 65

tightrope 25, 59, 99
transfer of learning **109**, 110, 118, 119
transfer of training 3, 4, 80, 91, 93, 103, 106, 108–110, 123
transformative learning 2, 3, 35, 72–80, 86–87, 90–91, 104–108, 114, 115, 117, 119, 122, 123
trust 1, 52, 107, 121–122, 125
turnover 44–45

urban school superintendent 1, 8, 11–12, 21, 23, 27, 29, 34–35, 36, 45, 58, 68, 81, 89, 93–94, 97, 99, 100, 102, 104–107, 115–116, 118, 125

vulnerable 39, 40, 42, 107

work avoidance 31
work-based-learning pyramid 108–110